Index: Financial Freedom Blueprint: Mastering Your Finances for Wealth and Security

Chapter 1: Understanding Your Financial Goals

- Setting Financial Objectives
- Short-Term vs. Long-Term Goals
- Prioritizing Financial Aspirations

Chapter 2: Assessing Your Risk Tolerance

- Defining Risk Tolerance
- Identifying Personal Risk Factors
- Matching Risk Tolerance to Investment Strategy

Chapter 3: Building a Solid Foundation

- Introduction to Asset Classes
- Stocks: Ownership and Growth
- Bonds: Fixed Income and Stability
- Cash: Liquidity and Safety
- Importance of Diversification

Chapter 4: Constructing Your Portfolio

- Selecting Specific Investments
- Asset Allocation Strategies
- Balancing Risk and Reward
- Conducting Thorough Research

Chapter 5: Monitoring and Adjusting Your Portfolio

- Establishing Monitoring Mechanisms
- Assessing Investment Performance
- Rebalancing Strategies
- Adapting to Changing Circumstances

Chapter 6: Tax Efficiency and Portfolio Management

- Understanding Tax Implications

- Tax-Efficient Investment Strategies
- Maximizing After-Tax Returns

Chapter 7: Reinvesting and Compounding

- The Power of Compounding
- Reinvesting Dividends and Interest
- Long-Term Growth Strategies

Chapter 8: Navigating Economic Challenges

- Staying Focused on Long-Term Goals
- Decision-Making During Market Volatility
- Capitalizing on Opportunities
- Resilience in Economic Downturns

Conclusion

- Summary of Key Takeaways
- Continuing Your Financial Education
- Wishing You a Prosperous Financial Future

Appendix: Additional Resources

- Recommended Books
- Online Tools and Platforms
- Financial Planning Services
- Investment Research Websites

Chapter 1: Understanding Your Financial Goals

Setting Financial Objectives

In the opening chapter of "Financial Freedom Blueprint: Mastering Your Finances for Wealth and Security," we embark on a crucial journey of self-discovery, exploring the intricate process of setting and defining your financial objectives. Before diving into the complexities of investment portfolios, it is imperative to establish a clear roadmap for your financial future. This chapter serves as the foundational pillar upon which your entire investment strategy will be built.

Key Elements:

- **Clarifying Your Vision:**
    - Begin by envisioning your life at different stages. What are your aspirations, both short-term and long-term? Visualize milestones such as purchasing a home, funding your children's education, or enjoying a comfortable retirement.
- **Identifying Priorities:**
    - Not all financial goals are created equal. Prioritize your objectives based on urgency, significance, and personal values. This could involve categorizing goals into immediate needs, intermediate objectives, and long-term visions.
- **Quantifying Your Goals:**
    - Assign specific, measurable, achievable, relevant, and time-bound (SMART) parameters to your financial goals. This approach transforms abstract desires into concrete targets, facilitating a more focused and actionable plan.
- **Assessing Risk Tolerance in Goal Setting:**
    - Consider the risk associated with each goal. Some objectives may require more aggressive investment strategies, while others may demand a conservative approach. Understanding your risk tolerance at this early stage will lay the groundwork for future investment decisions.
- **Aligning with Values:**
    - Your financial goals should align with your values and lifestyle. Reflect on what truly matters to you, ensuring that your financial plan is a reflection of your beliefs, ethics, and long-term vision.

Practical Exercises:

- **Goal Visualization Exercise:**

- Engage in a guided visualization exercise to vividly imagine achieving your financial goals. This can provide emotional motivation and clarity.
- **Prioritization Matrix:**
  - Create a matrix to categorize and prioritize your financial goals based on urgency and significance. This will serve as a practical tool for decision-making.
- **Risk Tolerance Assessment:**
  - Utilize self-assessment tools or professional advice to gauge your risk tolerance, providing a crucial framework for aligning investment strategies with your goals.

By the end of this chapter, you will have a crystal-clear understanding of your financial aspirations, paving the way for the subsequent chapters that delve into the strategic and tactical aspects of building your own investment portfolio.

Chapter 1: Understanding Your Financial Goals

Short-Term vs. Long-Term Goals

In the second point of Chapter 1, "Financial Freedom Blueprint: Mastering Your Finances for Wealth and Security" delves into the critical distinction between short-term and long-term financial goals. Recognizing and comprehending the temporal nature of your objectives is essential for effective financial planning, as it forms the basis for developing a strategy that aligns with the time horizon of each goal.

Key Elements:

- **Defining Short-Term Goals:**
  - Short-term goals typically span one to three years and often involve immediate financial needs or foreseeable life changes. These may include building an emergency fund, saving for a vacation, or making a down payment on a home.
- **Envisioning Long-Term Objectives:**
  - Long-term goals extend beyond three years and encompass major life events such as homeownership, funding education, and retirement planning. These objectives require a more sustained and disciplined approach to financial management.
- **Understanding Time Horizon Impacts:**
  - The time horizon of a goal profoundly influences the investment strategy applied to achieve it. Short-term goals may involve more conservative investments to preserve capital, while long-term goals can benefit from a

more growth-oriented approach with the ability to weather market fluctuations.
- **Balancing Short-Term Needs with Long-Term Vision:**
  - Striking a balance between immediate financial needs and long-term aspirations is crucial. This chapter guides you through the process of allocating resources effectively to address short-term obligations without compromising the pursuit of significant, future-oriented goals.
- **Adjusting Strategies for Each Horizon:**
  - Recognizing the different dynamics at play in short-term versus long-term investments, this section provides insights into tailoring your investment strategies accordingly. Whether it's creating liquidity for short-term needs or capitalizing on compounding for long-term growth, adapting your approach is key.

Practical Exercises:

- **Goal Time-Frame Mapping:**
  - Create a timeline for each financial goal, marking the distinction between short-term and long-term objectives. This visualization aids in understanding the time horizon associated with each aspiration.
- **Risk Assessment for Each Goal:**
  - Evaluate the risk tolerance and risk capacity specific to short-term and long-term goals. This exercise helps in determining the appropriate level of risk for each investment in the portfolio.
- **Prioritizing Funding Allocation:**
  - Develop a funding allocation plan that prioritizes short-term needs without compromising the progress toward long-term goals. This hands-on exercise provides a practical approach to balancing conflicting financial demands.

Chapter 1: Understanding Your Financial Goals

Prioritizing Financial Aspirations

In the third point of Chapter 1, "Financial Freedom Blueprint: Mastering Your Finances for Wealth and Security" continues the exploration of goal setting by delving into the essential process of prioritizing financial aspirations. This aspect is fundamental in guiding your decision-making, ensuring that you allocate resources efficiently to achieve the most significant impact on your financial well-being.

Key Elements:

- **Hierarchical Goal Setting:**
    - Establish a hierarchy among your financial goals, recognizing those that hold the highest priority. Whether it's paying off high-interest debt, building an emergency fund, or saving for a down payment on a home, this section guides you in organizing your objectives in order of importance.
- **Evaluating Urgency and Impact:**
    - Assess the urgency and impact of each goal on your overall financial health. Urgent goals may demand immediate attention, while high-impact goals could significantly improve your financial situation in the long run. Balancing these factors is crucial in crafting a well-rounded financial plan.
- **Financial Independence and Freedom:**
    - Consider the goals that contribute to financial independence and freedom. These might include eliminating debt, establishing a robust emergency fund, and securing your retirement. Prioritizing goals that enhance your financial freedom lays the groundwork for a more secure and fulfilling future.
- **Adapting to Changing Circumstances:**
    - Recognize that life is dynamic, and circumstances may evolve over time. This section provides guidance on adapting your priorities in response to changing financial situations, career advancements, or unexpected challenges.
- **Aligning Values with Priorities:**
    - Ensure that your prioritization aligns with your values and long-term vision. This process helps in fostering a sense of purpose and commitment to your financial goals, making it more likely that you'll stay dedicated to your financial plan.

Practical Exercises:

- **Priority Matrix:**
    - Create a matrix that combines urgency and impact to visually represent the priority of each financial goal. This exercise aids in making informed decisions about where to allocate resources first.
- **Values Alignment Checklist:**
    - Develop a checklist to evaluate how well each goal aligns with your personal values. This introspective exercise ensures that your financial priorities resonate with your core beliefs.
- **Dynamic Goal Adjustment:**
    - Establish a framework for periodically reviewing and adjusting your financial priorities. Life changes, and so should your goals. This exercise provides a practical approach to staying agile in your financial planning.

Chapter 2: Assessing Your Risk Tolerance

Defining Risk Tolerance

In the opening point of Chapter 2, "Financial Freedom Blueprint: Mastering Your Finances for Wealth and Security" takes a deep dive into the intricate concept of risk tolerance—a fundamental aspect of understanding oneself as an investor. Risk tolerance refers to an individual's willingness and ability to endure fluctuations in the value of their investments with the aim of achieving long-term financial objectives. This nuanced exploration aims to provide readers with a comprehensive understanding of risk, paving the way for informed and strategic investment decisions.

Key Elements:

- **Psychological and Emotional Dimensions:**
    - Risk tolerance is inherently tied to one's emotional and psychological makeup. This section delves into the emotional aspects of investing, exploring how personal experiences, fears, and attitudes towards money can shape an individual's tolerance for financial risk.
- **Volatility and Market Fluctuations:**
    - Understanding the inherent unpredictability of financial markets is crucial. This point elucidates the nature of market volatility and how it can impact investment portfolios, influencing an investor's comfort level with risk.
- **Financial Capacity for Risk:**
    - Beyond emotional considerations, risk tolerance involves a practical assessment of one's financial capacity to withstand losses. This section guides readers in evaluating their financial circumstances, including income, expenses, and emergency savings, to determine the extent to which they can bear financial risks.
- **Time Horizon and Risk:**
    - The relationship between time and risk is explored, emphasizing that risk tolerance is not a static attribute but evolves over an individual's investment horizon. Younger investors with longer time horizons may be more tolerant of short-term market fluctuations compared to those nearing retirement.
- **Risk Tolerance Assessment Tools:**

- This chapter introduces readers to various risk tolerance assessment tools and methodologies. From questionnaires that probe personal attitudes toward risk to scenario-based assessments, these tools aid in quantifying risk tolerance and informing strategic investment choices.

Practical Exercises:

- **Emotional Risk Reflection:**
    - Readers are encouraged to reflect on their emotional responses to financial situations, identifying patterns of behavior that may indicate their emotional tolerance for risk.
- **Scenario Analysis:**
    - Engage in scenario analysis exercises that simulate different market conditions and assess the emotional and financial responses to potential risks.
- **Risk Tolerance Questionnaires:**
    - Complete risk tolerance questionnaires provided in the book, helping readers quantify their risk tolerance and gain insights into their comfort levels with various investment scenarios.

Chapter 2: Assessing Your Risk Tolerance

Identifying Personal Risk Factors

In the second point of Chapter 2, "Financial Freedom Blueprint: Mastering Your Finances for Wealth and Security" dives deeper into the multifaceted concept of risk tolerance by exploring the various personal factors that can influence an individual's willingness and ability to take on financial risks. This section aims to provide readers with a nuanced understanding of how their unique circumstances, beliefs, and life situations contribute to their overall risk tolerance.

Key Elements:

- **Financial Knowledge and Experience:**
  - The level of financial knowledge and investment experience significantly impacts risk tolerance. This section delves into how a solid understanding of financial markets and investment instruments can boost confidence and potentially influence risk-taking behavior.
- **Career Stability and Income:**
  - Job stability and income play pivotal roles in shaping risk tolerance. Readers are guided through an exploration of how a secure job and a consistent income stream can positively impact an individual's willingness to take on financial risks.
- **Debt Levels and Financial Obligations:**
  - The extent of personal debt and financial obligations is explored as a crucial determinant of risk tolerance. High levels of debt may reduce one's capacity to take on additional financial risks, while a more stable financial position may allow for a higher tolerance.
- **Life Stage and Responsibilities:**
  - Different life stages bring varying levels of responsibility and financial commitment. This section examines how factors such as marriage, parenthood, and homeownership can influence an individual's risk tolerance, as these life events often come with increased financial responsibilities.
- **Psychological Factors:**
  - Delving into the psychological aspects of risk, this segment explores how individual attitudes towards uncertainty, fear of loss, and the desire for financial security contribute to one's overall risk tolerance.

Practical Exercises:

- **Financial Knowledge Self-Assessment:**

- o Readers are encouraged to assess their own financial knowledge and identify areas for improvement. Resources and suggestions for expanding financial literacy are provided.
- **Debt-to-Income Ratio Analysis:**
  - o A practical exercise involves evaluating the current debt-to-income ratio, providing insight into how existing financial obligations may impact risk tolerance.
- **Life Stage Reflection:**
  - o Readers are prompted to reflect on their current life stage, recognizing how personal responsibilities and commitments may influence their comfort level with financial risk.

Chapter 2: Assessing Your Risk Tolerance

Matching Risk Tolerance to Investment Strategy

In the third point of Chapter 2, "Financial Freedom Blueprint: Mastering Your Finances for Wealth and Security" continues the exploration of risk tolerance, focusing on the pivotal aspect of aligning one's risk tolerance with an appropriate investment strategy. Understanding how personal comfort levels with risk can harmonize with specific investment approaches is crucial for creating a portfolio that reflects individual preferences and goals.

Key Elements:

- **Conservative vs. Aggressive Strategies:**
    - This section delves into the spectrum of investment strategies, ranging from conservative to aggressive. Readers are guided through an exploration of how risk tolerance influences the choice between safer, lower-return investments and riskier, potentially higher-return options.
- **Diversification and Risk Mitigation:**
    - The concept of diversification is introduced as a powerful risk management tool. Readers learn how spreading investments across different asset classes can moderate risk and enhance the stability of a portfolio, irrespective of an individual's risk tolerance.
- **Risk-Return Relationship:**
    - The inherent relationship between risk and return is elucidated, emphasizing that higher potential returns often come with increased volatility and risk. This section assists readers in finding a balanced approach that aligns with their risk tolerance while striving to meet financial goals.
- **Understanding Volatility:**
    - Volatility, a measure of how much an investment's value fluctuates, is discussed in detail. Readers gain insights into how volatility can impact investment decisions and how different levels of volatility may suit varying risk tolerances.
- **Customizing Portfolios to Risk Profiles:**
    - This segment explores the process of tailoring investment portfolios to match individual risk profiles. Whether constructing a conservative portfolio with a focus on capital preservation or an aggressive portfolio with growth as the primary goal, readers will learn how to make strategic choices.

Practical Exercises:

- **Risk-Return Assessment:**
    - Readers engage in a risk-return assessment exercise, evaluating their comfort levels with different risk and return scenarios to identify an appropriate balance.

- **Diversification Simulation:**
    - A practical exercise involves simulating the impact of diversification on a portfolio, allowing readers to witness firsthand how this strategy can moderate risk.
- **Portfolio Customization Worksheet:**
    - Readers are provided with a worksheet to help customize their portfolios based on their risk tolerance, incorporating a mix of asset classes and investment vehicles.

Chapter 2: Assessing Your Risk Tolerance

Balancing Risk Tolerance with Investment Goals

In the third point of Chapter 2, "Financial Freedom Blueprint: Mastering Your Finances for Wealth and Security" delves into the intricate process of balancing risk tolerance with specific investment goals. Recognizing that risk tolerance is not a one-size-fits-all concept, this section guides readers in understanding how to tailor their risk exposure based on the objectives they aim to achieve.

Key Elements:

- **Defining Investment Goals:**
    - The chapter commences by emphasizing the importance of clearly defining investment goals. Whether the objective is wealth accumulation for retirement, funding education, or purchasing a home, each goal carries its own risk considerations.
- **Risk-Return Optimization:**
    - Readers are introduced to the concept of risk-return optimization, emphasizing the need to align risk-taking with the potential returns required to achieve specific financial objectives. This section provides practical insights into finding the delicate balance that suits individual goals.
- **Short-Term vs. Long-Term Objectives:**
    - The time horizon of investment goals plays a crucial role in determining the appropriate level of risk. This point navigates the distinctions between short-term and long-term objectives, guiding readers in adjusting risk exposure based on the time frame of their goals.
- **Risk Management Strategies:**
    - Various risk management strategies are explored, offering readers tools to mitigate potential downsides while maintaining a realistic approach to achieving their investment goals. Techniques such as stop-loss orders, hedging, and regular portfolio rebalancing are discussed.
- **Reevaluating Goals and Risk Tolerance:**
    - Recognizing that goals and risk tolerance can evolve over time, this section encourages readers to periodically reassess their financial objectives and comfort levels with risk. Adjusting the investment strategy accordingly is vital for staying on course toward financial success.

Practical Exercises:

- **Goal-Specific Risk Assessment:**
    - Readers engage in a goal-specific risk assessment exercise, evaluating the level of risk they are willing to undertake for each investment goal. This process helps in aligning risk tolerance with the unique requirements of each objective.
- **Time Horizon Reflection:**
    - A reflection exercise prompts readers to consider the time horizons associated with their goals, guiding them in making informed decisions about risk exposure based on the specific time frames of their objectives.
- **Regular Goal Review Checklist:**

- Readers are provided with a checklist to facilitate regular reviews of their investment goals and risk tolerance. This tool aids in adapting the investment strategy as circumstances change.

Chapter 3: Introduction to Asset Classes

Unveiling the Foundation of Investing

In the enlightening journey through "Financial Freedom Blueprint: Mastering Your Finances for Wealth and Security," Chapter 3 serves as a pivotal gateway, introducing readers to the cornerstone of investment strategies – asset classes. This chapter provides an extensive exploration of various asset classes, shedding light on their unique characteristics, risk-return profiles, and the crucial role they play in constructing a well-balanced investment portfolio.

Key Elements:

- **Defining Asset Classes:**
    - The chapter opens with a fundamental definition of asset classes. Asset classes are categories of financial instruments that share similar characteristics and are subject to the same laws and regulations. Common asset classes include stocks, bonds, cash equivalents, real estate, and alternative investments.
- **Stocks: Ownership in Companies:**
    - Delving into the world of equities, or stocks, readers gain an understanding of what it means to own a share in a company. The potential for capital appreciation, dividends, and voting rights are explored, along with the associated risks of market volatility.
- **Bonds: Fixed Income and Stability:**
    - The chapter then transitions to fixed-income securities, or bonds, elucidating how they provide investors with a predictable stream of income through interest payments. The concepts of maturity, credit quality, and interest rate risk are thoroughly examined.
- **Cash Equivalents: Liquidity and Safety:**
    - Cash equivalents, such as money market instruments, are presented as essential components of a portfolio. Readers learn how these assets offer liquidity, safety, and stability, serving as a valuable resource for meeting short-term financial needs.
- **Real Estate: Tangible Investments:**
    - Real estate, both physical properties and real estate investment trusts (REITs), is explored as an asset class providing diversification and the potential for appreciation. Readers gain insights into the unique characteristics and considerations associated with real estate investments.
- **Alternative Investments: Diversification Beyond Tradition:**
    - The chapter concludes with a glimpse into alternative investments, encompassing commodities, hedge funds, and private equity. These assets offer diversification benefits and can act as a counterbalance to traditional asset classes.

Practical Examples:

- **Simulated Investment Portfolio:**
    - Readers are guided through the creation of a simulated investment portfolio, incorporating different asset classes. This hands-on exercise helps in understanding the impact of each asset class on the overall risk and return profile.
- **Historical Performance Analysis:**
    - Historical performance data of various asset classes is presented, allowing readers to observe how different classes have behaved in diverse market conditions. This analysis aids in forming expectations for future performance.
- **Risk-Return Matrix:**
    - A risk-return matrix is introduced, providing a visual representation of the risk and return characteristics of each asset class. This tool assists readers

in aligning their investment choices with their risk tolerance and financial goals.

Chapter 3 Stocks: Ownership and Growth

Unlocking the Power of Equities

In the financial landscape, stocks stand as pillars of ownership, embodying the essence of capitalism and wealth creation. In this section, we embark on a journey through the captivating world of stocks, unraveling the dynamics of ownership and growth.

- **Ownership in Companies:**
    - At its core, owning a stock means having a stake in a company, becoming a partial owner. Shareholders, as owners, hold voting rights in major company decisions, reflecting the democratic nature of corporate governance. This sense of ownership fosters a connection between investors and the companies they support.
- **Capital Appreciation:**
    - The allure of stocks lies in their potential for capital appreciation. As companies grow and prosper, so does the value of their shares. Investors witness their initial investments multiply, capturing the essence of wealth creation through ownership in successful enterprises.

- **Dividends as a Shareholder Reward:**
    - Beyond capital appreciation, stocks often reward investors through dividends. Companies distribute a portion of their profits to shareholders as dividends, providing a steady income stream. Dividends not only serve as a tangible return on investment but also reflect the financial health and stability of the company.
- **Risk and Volatility:**
    - However, the path to growth is not without challenges. Stocks are inherently volatile, subject to market fluctuations, economic shifts, and company-specific events. Investors navigate this volatility, understanding that the potential for reward is intricately linked with an acceptance of risk.

Real Case Description:

Case Study: Amazon (AMZN)

Amazon, the e-commerce behemoth founded by Jeff Bezos, offers a compelling real-world example of the power of stocks.

- **Ownership in a Global Giant:**
    - Investors who purchased Amazon shares during its initial public offering (IPO) in 1997 became part-owners of a fledgling online bookstore. As Amazon evolved into a global e-commerce giant, these investors experienced unparalleled ownership in a company that redefined retail.
- **Capital Appreciation:**
    - Amazon's stock price surged over the years, driven by its expansion into various sectors, including cloud computing (Amazon Web Services), streaming services (Amazon Prime Video), and artificial intelligence (Alexa). Investors witnessed significant capital appreciation as the stock price soared.
- **No Dividends, But Growth Potential:**
    - Interestingly, Amazon historically reinvested its profits into expansion and innovation rather than paying dividends. This strategy aligns with the growth-oriented nature of many technology companies. Investors accepted the absence of dividends, recognizing that the focus was on long-term value creation.
- **Volatility Amid Innovation:**
    - Amazon's journey has not been without volatility. Periods of market uncertainty and skepticism surrounded the company's ambitious initiatives. Yet, investors who understood the company's long-term vision and embraced the inherent volatility have been rewarded handsomely.

Practical Insights:

- **Diversification Strategy:**
    - While Amazon exemplifies the potential of individual stocks, prudent investors often adopt a diversified approach. Investing in a variety of stocks across different industries helps mitigate the risk associated with the performance of any single company.

- **Long-Term Perspective:**
    - The Amazon case study underscores the importance of adopting a long-term perspective when investing in stocks. Successful stock ownership often requires patience, allowing companies the time to innovate, adapt, and grow.

Dividend Stock Case Study: Johnson & Johnson (JNJ) - A Dividend Aristocrat

Harvesting Wealth through Steady Dividends and Aristocratic Stability

In the realm of dividend stocks, Johnson & Johnson (JNJ) not only stands as a pillar of stability but also earns the prestigious designation of a "Dividend Aristocrat." This case study delves into the enduring appeal of dividend stocks, exploring the historical track record of JNJ's dividends and elucidating the significance of being a Dividend Aristocrat.

1. A Pillar of Stability:

- Johnson & Johnson, established in 1886, has evolved into a diversified healthcare giant. Its resilience in navigating the dynamic healthcare sector positions it as a symbol of stability. This stability forms the foundation for its ability to consistently reward shareholders through dividends.

2. Consistent Dividend Payments:

- JNJ's commitment to shareholders is exemplified by over 50 consecutive years of annual dividend increases. This remarkable track record is a testament to the company's financial strength, robust business model, and dedication to providing shareholders with a reliable income stream.

3. Dividend Yield and Income Stream:

- Beyond the consistent payments, JNJ's dividend yield, a key metric representing the annual dividend income as a percentage of the stock price, is a factor that attracts income-oriented investors. The stock's yield has historically been competitive, providing shareholders with an attractive income stream.

4. Resilience in Economic Downturns:

- The healthcare sector's defensive nature has contributed to JNJ's resilience during economic downturns. This stability not only provides investors with a sense of security but also positions the stock as a defensive holding that can weather market volatility.

5. Reinvesting Dividends for Compound Growth:

- JNJ's dividend reinvestment plan (DRIP) allows investors to automatically reinvest dividends to acquire additional shares. This strategy leverages the power of compounding, enabling shareholders to accumulate more shares over time and potentially accelerate wealth growth.

6. The Aristocratic Distinction:

- Beyond being a dividend-paying stalwart, Johnson & Johnson holds the prestigious title of a Dividend Aristocrat. This distinction is bestowed upon companies that have not only paid dividends consistently but have also increased them for at least 25 consecutive years. JNJ's status as a Dividend Aristocrat reflects a rare level of commitment to shareholder value.

Real-World Impact:

Investor Perspective:

Returning to Sarah, the investor who purchased JNJ shares a decade ago:

- **Steady Income Stream:**
    - Sarah's reliance on JNJ's dividends for a steady income during retirement is complemented by the assurance that this income is part of a long-standing tradition of reliability.
- **Dividend Aristocrat Status:**
    - The fact that JNJ is a Dividend Aristocrat adds an extra layer of confidence for Sarah. The company's extended history of increasing dividends demonstrates not just stability but a commitment to sustained growth, aligning with her long-term investment goals.
- **Aristocratic Stability in Volatility:**
    - During market downturns, the aristocratic stability of JNJ shines through. The company's ability to maintain and increase dividends even in challenging times provides Sarah with a sense of security, assuring her that the aristocratic tradition of rewarding shareholders endures.

Practical Insights:

- **Dividend Aristocrats vs. Others:**
    - The distinction between Dividend Aristocrats and other dividend-paying stocks lies in the longevity of dividend growth. While many companies pay dividends, Aristocrats demonstrate an exceptional commitment by consistently increasing payouts for an extended period, signaling financial strength and management confidence.
- **Risk Mitigation with Aristocrats:**
    - Dividend Aristocrats are often considered resilient during market downturns. Their ability to sustain and increase dividends, even in adverse conditions, can act as a risk mitigation strategy for investors seeking stability in their portfolios.

Chapter 3: Bonds - Fixed Income and Stability

Unlocking the Power of Fixed-Income Investments

In the expansive landscape of investment options, bonds emerge as a cornerstone of stability and fixed income. Chapter 3 delves into the realm of bonds, unraveling their intricacies and highlighting their role in providing investors with a reliable income stream and a cushion of stability in their portfolios.

1. Understanding Bonds:

- Bonds, often referred to as fixed-income securities, represent loans made by investors to governments, municipalities, or corporations. When an investor purchases a bond, they essentially lend money to the bond issuer in exchange for periodic interest payments and the return of the principal amount at maturity.

2. Fixed Income in a Dynamic World:

- The term "fixed income" stems from the predictable nature of bond investments. Unlike stocks, where returns are subject to market fluctuations, bonds offer a fixed interest rate, providing investors with a known and regular income stream. This characteristic makes bonds a valuable asset for those seeking stability in their investment portfolios.

3. Sources of Fixed Income:

- The fixed income from bonds primarily comes in the form of interest payments. These payments are typically made semi-annually and are calculated as a percentage of the bond's face value. Additionally, when the bond reaches maturity, investors receive the principal amount back, offering a final source of fixed income.

4. Types of Bonds:

- Bonds come in various forms, including government bonds, municipal bonds, corporate bonds, and Treasury bonds. Each type has its own risk-return profile, with government bonds often considered the safest, backed by the full faith and credit of the government, and corporate bonds offering higher yields but with additional risk.

5. Rating Agencies and Risk Assessment:

- Bond investments are assessed for risk by credit rating agencies such as Moody's, Standard & Poor's, and Fitch. These agencies assign credit ratings based on the issuer's creditworthiness, helping investors gauge the level of risk associated with a particular bond.

Real-World Application:

Case Study: U.S. Treasury Bonds

Consider U.S. Treasury bonds, widely recognized for their stability and reliability.

- **Fixed Interest Payments:**

- o An investor purchases a 10-year U.S. Treasury bond with a face value of $10,000 and an annual interest rate of 2%. This means the investor will receive fixed interest payments of $200 per year for the next 10 years.
- **Return of Principal at Maturity:**
  - o At the end of the 10-year period, the investor receives the face value of the bond, totaling $10,000. This return of principal provides a final source of fixed income.
- **Government Backing and Safety:**
  - o U.S. Treasury bonds are considered among the safest investments because they are backed by the full faith and credit of the U.S. government. This safety net contributes to the stability of the fixed-income stream.

Practical Insights:

- **Diversification with Bonds:**
  - o Bonds play a crucial role in diversifying a portfolio. Their stable and predictable returns can offset the volatility often associated with stocks, providing a balanced investment approach.
- **Interest Rate Risk:**
  - o Investors should be aware of interest rate risk, which arises when interest rates in the broader economy change. Existing bonds may lose value if newly issued bonds offer higher interest rates. Understanding this risk is essential for bond investors.
- **Bond Laddering Strategy:**
  - o Investors can implement a bond laddering strategy, spreading investments across bonds with different maturities. This approach helps manage interest rate risk and provides a consistent income stream.

By exploring the world of bonds, investors gain insights into the power of fixed income and stability. Bonds, with their regular interest payments and return of principal, offer a reliable foundation for constructing well-balanced portfolios suited to various investment goals and risk tolerances.

Credit rating agencies play a crucial role in assessing the creditworthiness of issuers of debt securities, such as governments, municipalities, and corporations. The ratings provided by these agencies help investors gauge the risk associated with specific bonds or other fixed-income instruments. Here are some prominent credit rating agencies and insights on how to interpret their ratings:

1. Moody's Investors Service:

- **Background:** Moody's is one of the oldest and most widely recognized credit rating agencies. It provides credit ratings, research, and risk analysis.
- **Ratings Scale:** Moody's uses a letter-based rating system ranging from "Aaa" for the highest quality to "C" for the lowest. The ratings are further divided into numerical subcategories (e.g., Aa1, Aa2, Aa3).

2. Standard & Poor's (S&P):

- **Background:** S&P is a leading global provider of credit ratings, research, and analytics. It is known for its comprehensive coverage of various financial markets.
- **Ratings Scale:** S&P employs a letter-based rating system, starting with "AAA" as the highest and descending to "D" for default. The plus and minus modifiers indicate gradations within each rating category.

3. Fitch Ratings:

- **Background:** Fitch is a global credit rating agency providing credit opinions on a wide range of entities, including sovereigns, corporates, and structured finance.
- **Ratings Scale:** Fitch uses a letter-based rating system similar to Moody's and S&P. Ratings range from "AAA" to "D," with plus and minus modifiers indicating finer distinctions within each category.

4. Kroll Bond Rating Agency (KBRA):

- **Background:** KBRA is a relatively newer player in the credit rating industry, known for its focus on new and innovative sectors. It aims to provide transparent and timely ratings.
- **Ratings Scale:** KBRA uses a letter-based rating system, similar to other agencies, ranging from "AAA" to "D."

Evaluating Credit Ratings:

- **Understanding the Scale:**
    - Familiarize yourself with the specific rating scales used by each agency. While they share similarities, nuances exist. For instance, an "A" rating from one agency might have a slightly different risk profile than an "A" from another.
- **Consider the Outlook and Watch Status:**
    - Agencies often provide an outlook (positive, stable, or negative) and watch status. These indicate the potential direction of a rating change. A "negative outlook" suggests a higher likelihood of a downgrade.
- **Use Multiple Sources:**
    - Rely on ratings from multiple agencies for a more comprehensive assessment. Discrepancies between ratings may reveal differing perspectives on an issuer's creditworthiness.
- **Supplement with Research:**
    - Credit ratings should be supplemented with additional research. Understand the rationale behind the rating, examine the issuer's financial health, and consider economic and industry factors.
- **Watch for Rating Changes:**

- o Keep an eye on rating changes. A downgrade can signal increased credit risk, potentially impacting the value of the related securities.
- **Consider Bond Covenants and Terms:**
  - o Evaluate not only the credit rating but also the specific terms and covenants of the bond. Some bonds may have protective covenants that provide additional security for investors.
- **Understand Limitations:**
  - o Recognize that credit ratings are opinions based on available information. They are not foolproof indicators, and unforeseen events can impact an issuer's creditworthiness.

By approaching credit ratings with a critical mindset, considering multiple sources, and conducting supplementary research, investors can make more informed decisions about fixed-income investments and manage their risk exposure effectively.

Deciding when to purchase corporate or government bonds involves considering various factors, including your investment objectives, risk tolerance, market conditions, and the economic environment. Here are some considerations for both types of bonds:

Corporate Bonds:

- **Economic Conditions:**
  - o Corporate bonds are influenced by economic conditions. During periods of economic growth, corporations may issue bonds to fund expansion. Conversely, economic downturns may lead to increased default risk. Consider economic indicators and forecasts when deciding to invest in corporate bonds.
- **Company Financial Health:**
  - o Assess the financial health of the issuing company. Review financial statements, debt levels, and credit ratings from agencies like Moody's, S&P, or Fitch. Strong, well-established companies with a solid track record may offer more reliable corporate bonds.

- **Interest Rate Environment:**
    - Corporate bond prices are inversely related to interest rates. In a rising interest rate environment, existing bonds may decrease in value. Consider the current interest rate environment and your outlook on interest rate movements when purchasing corporate bonds.
- **Credit Ratings:**
    - Pay attention to credit ratings assigned by rating agencies. Higher-rated bonds generally have lower default risk but may offer lower yields. Balance your risk tolerance with the desire for higher yields.
- **Industry Trends:**
    - Understand industry trends and the specific dynamics of the sector in which the company operates. Certain industries may be more susceptible to economic fluctuations or regulatory changes, affecting the performance of corporate bonds within those sectors.

Government Bonds:

- **Interest Rate Movements:**
    - Government bonds, particularly those issued by developed countries, are influenced by central bank interest rate policies. Monitor central bank decisions and interest rate trends to gauge the impact on government bond prices.
- **Inflation Expectations:**
    - Government bonds are sensitive to inflation. If you expect inflation to rise, consider purchasing Treasury Inflation-Protected Securities (TIPS), which adjust for inflation. These can protect your investment's purchasing power.
- **Country-Specific Risks:**
    - Assess the economic and political stability of the country issuing the bonds. Government bonds from economically stable and fiscally responsible countries are generally considered safer.
- **Yield Curve:**
    - Examine the yield curve for government bonds. A normal or upward-sloping yield curve indicates a healthy economy, while an inverted curve may signal economic concerns. Adjust your investment strategy based on your interpretation of the yield curve.
- **Risk-Free vs. Credit Risk Trade-off:**
    - Government bonds are often considered low-risk, especially those issued by developed countries. The trade-off is lower yields compared to riskier assets. Evaluate your need for safety versus your desire for higher returns when deciding to invest in government bonds.

General Considerations:

- **Diversification:**
    - Diversify your bond portfolio to spread risk. Combining both corporate and government bonds can help achieve a balanced and diversified fixed-income allocation.
- **Investment Horizon:**

- o Consider your investment horizon. If you need liquidity in the short term, shorter-maturity government bonds might be more suitable. For long-term goals, a mix of corporate and government bonds may be appropriate.
- **Market Timing:**
  - o Timing the market can be challenging. Instead of trying to predict interest rate movements or economic cycles, focus on a disciplined, long-term investment strategy that aligns with your financial goals.

Chapter 3: Cash - Liquidity and Safety

Preserving Capital with Liquid Assets

In the financial landscape, cash stands as a bedrock of liquidity and safety. Chapter 4 delves into the crucial role of cash in an investment portfolio, elucidating how its liquidity and safety attributes contribute to capital preservation and strategic financial planning.

1. The Essence of Cash:

- At its core, cash is the most liquid asset, representing physical currency or its digital equivalent. It serves as a medium of exchange, providing immediate purchasing power and flexibility.

2. Liquidity - The Power to Act:

- Liquidity is the hallmark of cash. It refers to the ease with which an asset can be bought or sold without causing a significant impact on its price. Cash, being the most liquid asset, empowers investors to swiftly capitalize on opportunities or meet unexpected financial needs.

3. Safety - A Haven in Uncertain Times:

- Safety is the other pillar of cash. While it may not generate returns like other investments, cash serves as a secure haven, shielding capital from market volatility. In times of economic uncertainty or market downturns, holding cash provides a protective buffer against potential losses.

4. Emergency Funds and Contingency Planning:

- Cash plays a vital role in creating emergency funds. These funds, held in easily accessible accounts, ensure that individuals and investors have a financial cushion to weather unforeseen circumstances, such as medical emergencies or job loss.

5. Opportunity Fund - Seizing the Moment:

- Beyond emergencies, having a portion of assets in cash creates an "opportunity fund." This fund allows investors to seize investment opportunities that may arise during market downturns when asset prices are attractive.

Real-World Application:

Practical Example: Emergency Fund

Consider Sarah, a prudent investor with an emergency fund consisting of three to six months' worth of living expenses in cash.

- **Liquidity in Action:**
    - Sarah's emergency fund is held in a highly liquid savings account. In case of an unexpected expense, she can access the cash immediately without worrying about market conditions or the need to sell investments at unfavorable prices.
- **Safety Net in Uncertain Times:**
    - The cash component of Sarah's emergency fund provides a safety net during uncertain times, such as a sudden job loss or medical emergency. Knowing that she has immediate access to funds brings peace of mind and financial security.
- **Capital Preservation:**
    - While the cash in the emergency fund may not generate significant returns, its primary purpose is capital preservation. In times of market volatility, Sarah's emergency fund remains unaffected, safeguarding the principal amount.

Practical Insights:

- **Balancing Liquidity and Returns:**
    - While cash is essential for liquidity and safety, finding the right balance with other investments is crucial. Holding too much cash for extended periods may lead to missed opportunities for returns and wealth growth.
- **Interest-Bearing Accounts:**
    - Consider utilizing interest-bearing accounts or money market funds for holding cash. While maintaining liquidity, these options offer a modest return, helping offset the impact of inflation.
- **Dynamic Asset Allocation:**
    - Adopt a dynamic asset allocation approach that adjusts the cash component based on market conditions and personal financial goals. In robust markets, cash levels may be lower, while they might increase during periods of uncertainty.
- **Strategic Use of Cash:**
    - Strategically deploy cash for opportunistic investments or to rebalance a portfolio during market fluctuations. This proactive approach enhances the overall efficiency of the investment strategy.

Conclusion:

By understanding and leveraging the liquidity and safety attributes of cash, investors like Sarah can navigate financial uncertainties with confidence. Cash, as a foundational element, not only preserves capital but also serves as a strategic tool for seizing opportunities and maintaining financial resilience in ever-changing market landscapes.

Chapter 3: Importance of Diversification

Dancing in Harmony: The Power of Diversification

In the intricate world of investing, diversification emerges as a symphony, harmonizing risk and return to create a resilient and balanced portfolio. Chapter 5 delves into the paramount importance of diversification, unraveling how this strategic approach enhances stability, mitigates risk, and propels investors toward their financial goals.

1. Defining Diversification:
- Diversification is the art of spreading investments across different asset classes, industries, geographical regions, and individual securities. It is the embodiment of the adage "don't put all your eggs in one basket."

2. Mitigating Risk:
- At its core, diversification is a risk management strategy. By holding a variety of investments, the impact of poor performance in one area is offset by potentially better performance in another. This mitigates the risk of significant losses associated with concentrated holdings.

3. Asset Class Diversification:
- Diversifying across asset classes, such as stocks, bonds, and cash equivalents, provides a buffer against the volatility inherent in individual markets. Different asset classes have unique risk-return profiles, and their performance may not be perfectly correlated.

4. Geographic and Industry Diversification:
- Geographic and industry diversification further enhances risk mitigation. Economic conditions can vary across regions, and industries may respond differently to market cycles. A diversified portfolio spreads exposure, reducing vulnerability to localized economic downturns or sector-specific challenges.

5. Individual Security Diversification:
- Even within asset classes, diversification at the individual security level is crucial. Holding a mix of individual stocks or bonds helps mitigate the risk associated with the performance of a single company or issuer.

Real-World Application:

Case Study: The Power of Diversification

Consider an investor, Alex, who holds a well-diversified portfolio comprising stocks, bonds, and real estate investment trusts (REITs).

- **Market Volatility and Stock Performance:**

- During a period of market volatility, the stock portion of Alex's portfolio experiences a temporary decline due to economic uncertainties. However, the impact on the overall portfolio is cushioned by the performance of other asset classes, such as bonds and REITs.
- **Bonds Provide Stability:**
  - The bond component of Alex's portfolio provides stability and a consistent income stream during the market turbulence. Bonds often act as a counterbalance to the potential volatility in the stock market.
- **REITs and Real Estate Diversification:**
  - The inclusion of REITs in the portfolio introduces diversification into real estate. Even if the stock market faces headwinds, the performance of real estate assets may follow a different trajectory, contributing to overall portfolio resilience.

Practical Insights:

- **Risk-Adjusted Returns:**
  - Diversification aims for optimal risk-adjusted returns. While it may not eliminate risk entirely, it seeks to achieve a balance where potential returns are maximized for a given level of risk.
- **Rebalancing for Discipline:**
  - Regularly rebalancing a diversified portfolio maintains the desired asset allocation. This disciplined approach involves selling assets that have outperformed and buying those that have underperformed, ensuring alignment with long-term investment goals.
- **Investor Psychology and Emotional Resilience:**
  - Diversification fosters emotional resilience. In times of market turbulence, investors with well-diversified portfolios are less likely to succumb to fear or panic, as the impact of any single market event is buffered by the broader composition of the portfolio.
- **Long-Term Wealth Building:**
  - Diversification is a key strategy for long-term wealth building. While it may not result in the highest short-term gains, its primary aim is to provide a stable and sustainable path toward achieving financial goals over an extended time horizon.

Conclusion:

In the tapestry of investment strategies, diversification emerges as the maestro orchestrating stability and growth. By spreading investments across various assets, diversification not only mitigates risk but also empowers investors to navigate the dynamic and unpredictable currents of the financial markets with resilience and confidence.

Chapter 4: Constructing Your Portfolio

Crafting Your Financial Canvas: The Art of Investment Selection and Asset Allocation

As you embark on the journey of constructing your investment portfolio, this chapter delves into the intricacies of selecting specific investments, formulating asset allocation strategies, and navigating the delicate balance between risk and reward. Armed with the tools of thorough research, you'll paint a financial masterpiece tailored to your goals.

1. Selecting Specific Investments:

Unveiling the Gems in the Market

- **Diversification in Equities:**
  - Delve into the world of equities with a diversified approach. Select individual stocks across different sectors and industries, balancing large-cap stability with the growth potential of mid and small caps.
- **Bond Selection and Maturity Matching:**
  - Choose bonds based on your risk tolerance and income needs. Consider a mix of government, corporate, and municipal bonds. Align the maturities with your investment horizon to manage interest rate risk.
- **Real Assets for Tangible Growth:**
  - Explore real assets like real estate investment trusts (REITs) and commodities. These can add a layer of diversification and inflation protection to your portfolio.
- **Cash and Cash Equivalents:**
  - Ensure a portion of your portfolio is allocated to cash or cash equivalents for liquidity and stability. Money market funds and short-term bonds can serve this purpose.

2. Asset Allocation Strategies:

Harmony in Variety: The Art of Allocation

- **Strategic Asset Allocation:**
  - Establish a long-term strategic asset allocation based on your financial goals and risk tolerance. Allocate percentages to equities, bonds, and other asset classes to create a well-balanced foundation.
- **Tactical Asset Allocation:**
  - Embrace tactical adjustments based on short-term market conditions. Shift allocations opportunistically to capitalize on market trends while staying aligned with your long-term strategy.
- **Dynamic Asset Allocation:**
  - Implement a dynamic approach that adapts to changing economic conditions. Regularly review your portfolio and make adjustments to align with evolving market dynamics and your investment objectives.

3. Balancing Risk and Reward:

The Tightrope of Risk Management

- **Risk Tolerance Assessment:**
  - Begin with a thorough assessment of your risk tolerance. Understand your comfort level with market fluctuations and potential losses. This forms the bedrock of your risk management strategy.
- **Correlation Analysis:**

- o Consider the correlation between different asset classes in your portfolio. Aim for assets that don't move in lockstep, enhancing the diversification benefits and minimizing overall portfolio risk.
- **Volatility Mitigation Strategies:**
  - o Integrate strategies to mitigate volatility, such as incorporating low-volatility stocks or employing options strategies. These measures can help smooth the overall risk profile of your portfolio.

4. Conducting Thorough Research:

The Beacon of Informed Decision-Making

- **Fundamental Analysis:**
  - o Dive into the fundamentals of individual stocks and bonds. Assess financial statements, earnings reports, and economic indicators to gauge the intrinsic value and potential growth of your investments.
- **Technical Analysis:**
  - o Leverage technical analysis tools to understand market trends, entry and exit points, and potential support/resistance levels. Technical analysis can complement fundamental research for a comprehensive view.
- **Economic and Market Research:**
  - o Stay abreast of economic indicators, market trends, and geopolitical events. A holistic understanding of the macroeconomic environment can inform your investment decisions and asset allocation choices.
- **Due Diligence on Investment Vehicles:**
  - o Thoroughly research investment vehicles such as mutual funds, exchange-traded funds (ETFs), and other financial instruments. Assess fees, historical performance, and alignment with your overall portfolio strategy.

Conclusion:

Embarking on the construction of your portfolio is both an art and a science. By carefully selecting specific investments, crafting robust asset allocation strategies, balancing risk and reward, and conducting thorough research, you lay the foundation for a resilient and purposeful financial canvas. As you navigate the dynamic landscape of the financial markets, this chapter serves as your guide, empowering you to make informed decisions and shape a portfolio that aligns seamlessly with your unique investment goals.

Let's create a simplified portfolio focusing on asset classes and their respective percentages for a 30-year-old with $20,000:

1. Domestic Equities (50%):

- Allocate 50% to a low-cost Total Stock Market Index Fund, providing broad exposure to U.S. large, mid, and small-cap stocks.

2. International Equities (20%):

- Dedicate 20% to an International Equity Fund or ETF for global diversification outside the United States.

3. **Bonds (20%):**

- Allocate 20% to a Diversified Bond Fund, incorporating various bond types like government, corporate, and municipal bonds for stability and income.

4. **Real Assets (10%):**

- Allocate 10% to a Real Estate Investment Trust (REIT) ETF for exposure to the real estate market.

Portfolio Summary:

- **Domestic Equities: 50%**
- **International Equities: 20%**
- **Bonds: 20%**
- **Real Assets (REITs): 10%**

This portfolio offers a balanced mix of asset classes, providing exposure to both domestic and international equities for growth potential, bonds for stability, and real assets for additional diversification. It reflects a moderate risk profile suitable for a 30-year-old with a long-term investment horizon.

let's specify some examples for each asset class in the portfolio:

1. **Domestic Equities (50%):**

- Allocate 50% to a low-cost Total Stock Market Index Fund, such as Vanguard Total Stock Market Index Fund (VTSMX) or a similar ETF like iShares Core S&P Total U.S. Stock Market ETF (ITOT). These funds aim to replicate the performance of the entire U.S. stock market.

2. **International Equities (20%):**

- Dedicate 20% to an International Equity Fund or ETF, such as Vanguard Total International Stock Index Fund (VGTSX) or iShares MSCI ACWI ex U.S. ETF (ACWX). These funds provide exposure to stocks outside the United States.

3. **Bonds (20%):**

- Allocate 20% to a Diversified Bond Fund, such as Vanguard Total Bond Market Index Fund (VBMFX) or iShares Core U.S. Aggregate Bond ETF (AGG). These funds encompass a mix of government, corporate, and other investment-grade bonds.

4. **Real Assets (10%):**

- Allocate 10% to a Real Estate Investment Trust (REIT) ETF, such as Vanguard Real Estate Index Fund (VGSLX) or iShares U.S. Real Estate ETF (IYR). These funds invest in a diversified portfolio of real estate-related assets.

Sample Portfolio with Specific Funds:

- **Domestic Equities (50%):**

- o   Vanguard Total Stock Market Index Fund (VTSMX) or iShares Core S&P Total U.S. Stock Market ETF (ITOT)
- **International Equities (20%):**
  - o   Vanguard Total International Stock Index Fund (VGTSX) or iShares MSCI ACWI ex U.S. ETF (ACWX)
- **Bonds (20%):**
  - o   Vanguard Total Bond Market Index Fund (VBMFX) or iShares Core U.S. Aggregate Bond ETF (AGG)
- **Real Assets (10%):**
  - o   Vanguard Real Estate Index Fund (VGSLX) or iShares U.S. Real Estate ETF (IYR)

As an individual approaches retirement, the investment strategy typically undergoes a shift to prioritize capital preservation and income generation while maintaining a level of growth to combat inflation. Here's a modified portfolio allocation for a 60-year-old close to retirement:

1. Domestic Equities (30%):

- Retain a portion in a Total Stock Market Index Fund or a mix of large-cap, dividend-paying stocks for potential growth.

2. International Equities (15%):

- Reduce exposure to international equities to 15% to manage risk, focusing on developed markets. Consider funds like Vanguard FTSE Developed Markets ETF (VEA) for international exposure.

3. Bonds (40%):

- Increase allocation to bonds to 40%, emphasizing stability and income. Include a mix of government and high-quality corporate bonds. Consider funds like Vanguard Total Bond Market Index Fund (VBTLX) or iShares iBoxx $ Investment Grade Corporate Bond ETF (LQD).

4. Real Assets (15%):

- Maintain exposure to real assets at 15%, focusing on income-generating real estate investment trusts (REITs). Consider Vanguard Real Estate Index Fund (VGSLX) or iShares U.S. Real Estate ETF (IYR).

Revised Sample Portfolio with Specific Funds for a 60-Year-Old:

- **Domestic Equities (30%):**
  - o   Vanguard Total Stock Market Index Fund (VTSMX) or a mix of individual dividend-paying stocks.
- **International Equities (15%):**
  - o   Vanguard FTSE Developed Markets ETF (VEA) or a similar international equity fund.
- **Bonds (40%):**

- o Vanguard Total Bond Market Index Fund (VBTLX) or iShares iBoxx $ Investment Grade Corporate Bond ETF (LQD).
- **Real Assets (15%):**
  - o Vanguard Real Estate Index Fund (VGSLX) or iShares U.S. Real Estate ETF (IYR).

Conclusion - Changes in Portfolio Allocation with Age:

As individuals progress through different life stages, their investment goals and risk tolerance evolve, leading to changes in portfolio allocation. Here are key considerations for changing portfolio allocation with age:

- **Risk Tolerance:**
  - o In early years, higher risk tolerance allows for a more aggressive allocation, emphasizing growth. As retirement approaches, a shift towards capital preservation becomes crucial to protect accumulated wealth.
- **Income Generation:**
  - o Younger investors may focus on capital appreciation, while retirees prioritize income generation. Increased allocation to bonds and dividend-paying stocks provides a reliable income stream during retirement.
- **Diversification:**
  - o Diversification remains essential throughout one's investment journey. However, the emphasis may shift from aggressive diversification in early years to a more balanced and conservative diversification close to retirement.
- **Capital Preservation:**
  - o Protecting capital becomes a priority for those nearing retirement. Greater emphasis on bonds, stable equities, and real assets helps minimize exposure to market volatility.
- **Inflation Protection:**
  - o Inflation erodes purchasing power over time. Including assets like TIPS and real estate can provide a hedge against inflation, ensuring that income generated in retirement keeps pace with rising living costs.
- **Regular Review and Adjustments:**
  - o Regularly reviewing and adjusting the portfolio is crucial. As retirement approaches, reassessments should occur to ensure the portfolio aligns with changing goals, risk tolerance, and market conditions.

In summary, portfolio allocation evolves with age, reflecting a balance between growth, income, and capital preservation. As individuals transition from the accumulation phase to retirement, the emphasis shifts towards more conservative investments, ensuring financial security and a reliable income stream during the golden years. Regular reviews and adjustments are essential to maintain a portfolio that aligns with changing life stages and financial objectives.

Asset allocation is a crucial aspect of constructing an investment portfolio, representing the distribution of your investments across various asset classes. The goal of asset allocation is to create a diversified portfolio that balances risk and return based on an investor's financial goals, risk tolerance, and time horizon. Here are some common asset allocation strategies:

- **Strategic Asset Allocation:**
    - **Definition:** Strategic asset allocation involves setting a predetermined long-term mix of asset classes that aligns with an investor's financial goals and risk tolerance.
    - **How It Works:** Investors establish a strategic allocation based on their risk preferences, financial goals, and time horizon. This allocation remains relatively unchanged over the long term, with periodic rebalancing to maintain the desired proportions.
    - **Example:** An investor may choose a strategic asset allocation of 60% stocks and 40% bonds based on their risk tolerance and financial objectives.
- **Tactical Asset Allocation:**
    - **Definition:** Tactical asset allocation involves making short-term adjustments to the portfolio based on market conditions and near-term expectations.
    - **How It Works:** Investors actively shift allocations in response to changes in economic conditions, market trends, or valuation metrics. This strategy aims to capitalize on short-term opportunities or mitigate potential risks.
    - **Example:** If an investor anticipates a market downturn, they might temporarily reduce equity exposure and increase allocations to more defensive assets.
- **Dynamic Asset Allocation:**
    - **Definition:** Dynamic asset allocation combines elements of both strategic and tactical approaches, allowing for adjustments based on changing economic conditions.
    - **How It Works:** Investors set a strategic asset allocation but make periodic adjustments in response to significant changes in market or economic conditions. This approach aims to capitalize on opportunities and manage risks in a changing investment landscape.

- o **Example:** If economic indicators signal a shift in market dynamics, an investor might adjust their asset allocation to better align with the evolving conditions.
- **Core-Satellite Asset Allocation:**
  - o **Definition:** Core-satellite asset allocation combines a core portfolio with strategic, tactical, or specialized satellite holdings.
  - o **How It Works:** The core portfolio consists of broad market index funds, providing stability and broad market exposure. Satellite holdings are additional, often more focused, investments that aim to enhance returns or manage risk.
  - o **Example:** The core might consist of a total stock market index fund, while satellite holdings could include sector-specific ETFs or actively managed funds with specialized strategies.
- **Life-Cycle or Target-Date Asset Allocation:**
  - o **Definition:** Life-cycle or target-date asset allocation adjusts over time based on an investor's changing time horizon, moving from a more aggressive to a more conservative mix as the target date (e.g., retirement) approaches.
  - o **How It Works:** Typically associated with retirement funds, these portfolios automatically shift allocations to reduce risk as the investor gets closer to the target date.
  - o **Example:** A target-date fund for someone planning to retire in 2035 might start with a more aggressive allocation in the early years and gradually shift to a more conservative mix as the target date approaches.

These asset allocation strategies provide a framework for investors to tailor their portfolios to meet specific financial objectives, risk preferences, and investment horizons. The right strategy often depends on individual circumstances, goals, and the level of involvement an investor wishes to have in managing their portfolio.

1. **Strategic Asset Allocation Portfolio with Nifty:**

- **Core Holdings (Long-Term):**
  - o 40%: Vanguard Total Stock Market Index Fund (VTSAX) - U.S. Equity
  - o 30%: iShares Core U.S. Aggregate Bond ETF (AGG) - U.S. Bonds
  - o 20%: Vanguard FTSE All-World ex-U.S. ETF (VEU) - International Equity (excluding India)
  - o 10%: Nifty 50 Index ETF (e.g., Nifty 50 ETF in India)

2. **Tactical Asset Allocation Portfolio with Nifty:**

- **Core Holdings (Long-Term):**
  - o 50%: Vanguard Total Stock Market Index Fund (VTSAX) - U.S. Equity
  - o 30%: iShares Core U.S. Aggregate Bond ETF (AGG) - U.S. Bonds
  - o 15%: Vanguard FTSE All-World ex-U.S. ETF (VEU) - International Equity (excluding India)
  - o 5%: Nifty 50 Index ETF

- **Tactical Adjustments (Short-Term):**
  - During periods of anticipated market downturns, consider shifting 10% from stocks to AGG and reallocating 5% from international equities to Nifty 50 for temporary risk reduction.

3. Dynamic Asset Allocation Portfolio with Nifty:

- **Core Holdings (Long-Term):**
  - 45%: Vanguard Total Stock Market Index Fund (VTSAX) - U.S. Equity
  - 30%: iShares Core U.S. Aggregate Bond ETF (AGG) - U.S. Bonds
  - 15%: Vanguard FTSE All-World ex-U.S. ETF (VEU) - International Equity (excluding India)
  - 10%: Nifty 50 Index ETF
- **Dynamic Adjustments (Periodic):**
  - Regularly review economic conditions. If there are signs of changing market dynamics, make adjustments to the allocation based on a dynamic approach, including the Nifty 50.

4. Core-Satellite Asset Allocation Portfolio with Nifty:

- **Core Holdings (Long-Term):**
  - 40%: Vanguard Total Stock Market Index Fund (VTSAX) - U.S. Equity
  - 25%: iShares Core U.S. Aggregate Bond ETF (AGG) - U.S. Bonds
  - 15%: Vanguard FTSE All-World ex-U.S. ETF (VEU) - International Equity (excluding India)
  - 10%: Nifty 50 Index ETF
- **Satellite Holdings (Enhanced Returns):**
  - 10%: Invesco India ETF (Pinvest - IN50) or another ETF that tracks the Nifty 50 index.

5. Life-Cycle or Target-Date Asset Allocation Portfolio with Nifty:

- **Target Date 2035 Portfolio:**
  - Vanguard Target Retirement 2035 Fund (VTTHX)
  - The allocation gradually shifts from a more aggressive mix to a more conservative mix as the target date approaches.
  - **Equity Holdings:**
    - 45%: Vanguard Total Stock Market Index Fund (VTSAX) - U.S. Equity
    - 20%: Vanguard FTSE All-World ex-U.S. ETF (VEU) - International Equity (excluding India)
    - 5%: Nifty 50 Index ETF
  - **Fixed Income Holdings:**
    - 30%: iShares Core U.S. Aggregate Bond ETF (AGG) - U.S. Bonds

Balancing risk and reward is a fundamental principle in investment management. Investors seek to optimize their portfolios to achieve the highest possible returns for a given level of risk or to minimize risk for a desired level of return. Here are key strategies for balancing risk and reward in your investment portfolio:

- **Diversification:**

- o **Risk Mitigation:** Diversification involves spreading investments across different asset classes, industries, and geographic regions. This helps reduce the impact of poor-performing assets on the overall portfolio.
  - o **Reward Potential:** While diversification doesn't eliminate risk, it can potentially enhance returns by capturing gains from various market segments.
- **Asset Allocation:**
  - o **Risk Mitigation:** Strategic asset allocation involves determining the optimal mix of asset classes based on your investment goals and risk tolerance. A well-balanced allocation can help manage risk during different market conditions.
  - o **Reward Potential:** Adjusting your asset allocation to include a mix of equities, bonds, and other asset classes allows you to participate in potential market gains while having stability from fixed-income assets.
- **Risk Tolerance Assessment:**
  - o **Risk Mitigation:** Understanding your risk tolerance helps align your investment choices with your comfort level. It prevents making emotionally-driven decisions during market volatility.
  - o **Reward Potential:** A higher risk tolerance may allow for a more aggressive allocation, potentially leading to higher returns. However, it's crucial to ensure alignment with your financial goals.
- **Correlation Analysis:**
  - o **Risk Mitigation:** Assessing the correlation between different assets in your portfolio helps identify how they move in relation to each other. Choosing assets with lower correlation can enhance diversification benefits.
  - o **Reward Potential:** Low correlation implies that assets may not move in tandem, potentially reducing overall portfolio volatility and enhancing risk-adjusted returns.
- **Volatility Mitigation Strategies:**
  - o **Risk Mitigation:** Implement strategies to mitigate volatility, such as incorporating low-volatility stocks or using options strategies. These strategies can help smooth out the ups and downs in your portfolio.
  - o **Reward Potential:** While volatility reduction may slightly limit upside potential, it can also protect against significant losses during market downturns.
- **Periodic Rebalancing:**
  - o **Risk Mitigation:** Regularly review and rebalance your portfolio to maintain the desired asset allocation. This ensures that your risk exposure doesn't drift too far from your original plan.
  - o **Reward Potential:** Rebalancing may involve selling some overperforming assets and buying underperforming ones, which can enhance returns over time.
- **Risk-Adjusted Return Metrics:**

- **Risk Mitigation:** Evaluate risk-adjusted return metrics like the Sharpe ratio, which considers the excess return per unit of risk. This helps assess whether your portfolio is providing sufficient return for the level of risk taken.
- **Reward Potential:** Aim for a balance where the portfolio's return justifies the level of risk assumed.

Chapter 4: Conducting Thorough Research

Conducting thorough research is essential when building and managing an investment portfolio. Successful investing requires a comprehensive understanding of various parameters to make informed decisions. Here are key parameters to focus on during the research process:

- **Investment Goals:**
  - Clearly define your short-term and long-term investment goals. Whether it's saving for a house, education, or retirement, understanding your objectives will guide your investment strategy.

- **Risk Tolerance:**
  - Assess your risk tolerance, which is your ability and willingness to withstand fluctuations in the value of your investments. Different asset classes come with varying levels of risk, and aligning your portfolio with your risk tolerance is crucial.
- **Time Horizon:**
  - Consider your time horizon for investment. The length of time until you need to access your funds will influence your asset allocation. Longer time horizons may allow for a more aggressive strategy.
- **Asset Allocation:**
  - Determine the appropriate mix of asset classes based on your goals, risk tolerance, and time horizon. Asset allocation is a critical factor influencing portfolio performance.
- **Market Conditions:**
  - Stay informed about current market conditions and economic trends. Understand the broader economic environment, interest rates, inflation expectations, and geopolitical factors that may impact investment markets.
- **Company Fundamentals (Stocks):**
  - If investing in individual stocks, analyze company fundamentals. This includes evaluating financial statements, earnings growth, dividends, competitive positioning, and the company's overall health.
- **Industry and Sector Analysis:**
  - Consider the performance and outlook of specific industries and sectors. Some sectors may outperform during certain economic conditions, and your portfolio should reflect this understanding.
- **Macroeconomic Indicators:**
  - Monitor macroeconomic indicators such as GDP growth, employment rates, inflation, and interest rates. These factors can influence the overall health of the economy and impact investment returns.
- **Valuation Metrics:**
  - Evaluate valuation metrics for individual securities or funds. Common metrics include price-to-earnings ratio (P/E), price-to-book ratio (P/B), and dividend yield. These metrics provide insights into whether an investment is overvalued or undervalued.
- **Historical Performance:**
  - Review the historical performance of assets or funds you are considering. Past performance is not indicative of future results, but it can provide insights into how an investment has weathered different market conditions.
- **Management Team (Mutual Funds/ETFs):**
  - If considering mutual funds or ETFs, assess the expertise and track record of the fund's management team. A skilled and experienced management team can contribute to the fund's overall success.
- **Fees and Expenses:**

- o Understand the fees and expenses associated with your investments. High fees can erode returns over time, so opt for cost-effective investment options.
- **Regulatory Environment:**
  - o Be aware of the regulatory environment in which you are investing. Changes in regulations can impact the performance and legality of certain investments.
- **ESG Considerations:**
  - o For socially responsible investing, consider Environmental, Social, and Governance (ESG) factors. Evaluate how well companies align with ethical and sustainability criteria.
- **Liquidity:**
  - o Assess the liquidity of the investments. Highly liquid assets can be easily bought or sold in the market without significantly impacting their price.

Let's delve deeper into the key valuation metrics:

- **Price-to-Earnings Ratio (P/E):**
  - **Calculation:** P/E ratio is calculated by dividing the market price per share by the earnings per share (EPS). $P/E\ Ratio = \dfrac{\text{Market Price per Share}}{\text{Earnings per Share (EPS)}}$
  - o **Significance:**
    - A high P/E ratio may indicate that the market has high expectations for future earnings growth.
    - A low P/E ratio could suggest that the market has lower expectations or that the stock may be undervalued.
    - Compare the P/E ratio to industry peers for a relative assessment.
- **Price-to-Book Ratio (P/B):**
  - **Calculation:** P/B ratio is calculated by dividing the market price per share by the book value per share. $P/B\ Ratio = \dfrac{\text{Market Price per Share}}{\text{Book Value per Share}}$
  - o **Significance:**
    - A high P/B ratio may indicate that the market values the company's assets and potential future earnings.
    - A low P/B ratio may suggest undervaluation or that the market has concerns about the company's future performance.
- **Dividend Yield:**
  - o **Calculation:** Dividend Yield is calculated by dividing the annual dividend per share by the market price per share, expressed as a percentage. $\text{Dividend Yield} = \dfrac{\text{Annual Dividend per Share}}{\text{Market Price per Share}} \times 100$
  - o **Significance:**
    - A high dividend yield may suggest that the stock is providing a relatively higher income stream compared to its market price.

- ▪ A low dividend yield may indicate that the stock is prioritizing capital appreciation over income.
- **Earnings Growth Rate:**
  - ○ **Calculation:** Earnings Growth Rate is the percentage increase in earnings over a specified period. $$\text{Earnings Growth Rate} = \frac{\text{Current Earnings} - \text{Previous Earnings}}{\text{Previous Earnings}} \times 100$$
  - ○ **Significance:**
    - ▪ A high earnings growth rate may justify a higher P/E ratio and suggest the potential for future appreciation.
    - ▪ Consistent earnings growth can be a positive sign for long-term investors.
- **PEG Ratio (Price/Earnings to Growth Ratio):**
  - ○ **Calculation:** PEG ratio is calculated by dividing the P/E ratio by the expected annual earnings growth rate. $$\text{PEG Ratio} = \frac{\text{P/E Ratio}}{\text{Earnings Growth Rate}}$$
  - ○ **Significance:**
    - ▪ PEG ratio accounts for earnings growth, providing a more comprehensive valuation metric.
    - ▪ A PEG ratio close to 1 suggests that the stock is reasonably valued based on its earnings growth.
- **Cash Flow Metrics (Free Cash Flow, Price-to-Cash Flow):**
  - ○ **Free Cash Flow (FCF):** It represents the cash generated by a company that is available for distribution to shareholders or reinvestment in the business.
  - ○ **Price-to-Cash Flow Ratio (P/CF):** Similar to P/E, it compares the market price to the company's cash flow per share.
  - ○ **Significance:**
    - ▪ Positive free cash flow indicates a company's ability to generate cash after covering its operating and capital expenses.
    - ▪ P/CF ratio can be used to assess how the market values the company's cash-generating capabilities.
- **Enterprise Value (EV) Metrics:**
  - ○ **Enterprise Value to Earnings (EV/E):** Compares the entire enterprise value to earnings.
  - ○ **Enterprise Value to EBITDA (EV/EBITDA):** Compares enterprise value to earnings before interest, taxes, depreciation, and amortization.
  - ○ **Significance:**
    - ▪ EV metrics provide a holistic view by considering a company's debt and cash positions in addition to market capitalization.
    - ▪ Useful for comparing companies with varying capital structures.
- **Relative Valuation Metrics (Comparative Analysis):**
  - ○ **Comparative Analysis:** Compare valuation metrics with industry peers, sector averages, or historical values for the same security.
  - ○ **Significance:**

- Relative valuation provides context by comparing the company's metrics to its peers or historical performance.
- Identifies whether a security is trading at a premium or discount relative to its counterparts.

When using valuation metrics, it's crucial to consider them in the context of the industry, economic conditions, and the company's specific circumstances.

Let's explore the concept of fees and expenses associated with investments in more detail:

- **Expense Ratios:**
    - **Definition:** The expense ratio represents the percentage of a fund's assets that are used to cover operating expenses. It includes management fees, administrative costs, and other operational expenses.
    - **Significance:**
        - Low expense ratios are generally favorable for investors as they result in a smaller portion of returns being consumed by fees.
        - Actively managed funds often have higher expense ratios compared to passively managed index funds or ETFs.
- **Front-End Loads and Back-End Loads:**
    - **Front-End Load:** A sales charge applied at the time of purchase.
    - **Back-End Load (Deferred Sales Charge):** A sales charge applied when an investor sells their shares.
    - **Significance:**
        - Loads represent fees paid to the fund's sales agents. They directly reduce the amount of money invested.
        - No-load funds do not charge these fees and may be more cost-effective for investors.
- **Transaction Costs:**
    - **Definition:** Transaction costs include brokerage commissions and other fees associated with buying and selling securities within a portfolio.
    - **Significance:**
        - Frequent trading can lead to higher transaction costs, impacting overall returns.
        - Passively managed index funds and ETFs often have lower turnover and associated transaction costs compared to actively managed funds.
- **Management Fees:**
    - **Definition:** Management fees are charges for the professional management of a fund's assets. These fees are typically expressed as an annual percentage of the fund's average net assets.
    - **Significance:**
        - Compare management fees across similar funds to ensure cost-effectiveness.

- - Passively managed funds often have lower management fees compared to actively managed funds.
- **Performance Fees (for Hedge Funds):**
  - **Definition:** Some hedge funds charge performance fees, which are a percentage of profits earned by the fund.
  - **Significance:**
    - Performance fees are in addition to management fees and can significantly impact overall costs.
    - Consider the impact of performance fees on returns, especially during strong market performance.
- **12b-1 Fees:**
  - **Definition:** 12b-1 fees are fees charged by some mutual funds to cover marketing and distribution expenses.
  - **Significance:**
    - These fees can contribute to a fund's overall expense ratio.
    - Funds with 12b-1 fees may have higher ongoing expenses.
- **Wrap Fees (for Managed Accounts):**
  - **Definition:** Wrap fees are comprehensive fees charged by investment advisors in managed accounts, covering advisory, transaction, and other expenses.
  - **Significance:**
    - While wrap fees provide a simplified fee structure, investors should understand the total cost and whether it aligns with the services provided.
- **Expense Caps and Fee Waivers:**
  - **Definition:** Some funds or investment products have expense caps or fee waivers, limiting the total expense ratio for a specified period.
  - **Significance:**
    - These arrangements can temporarily reduce costs for investors.
    - Be aware of the duration of fee waivers and the potential for expenses to increase after the waiver period.
- **Comparative Analysis:**
  - **Definition:** Compare fees and expenses of similar funds or investment options to identify cost-effective choices.
  - **Significance:**
    - Understanding how fees compare can aid in selecting investments with competitive cost structures.
    - Consider the impact of fees on long-term returns.
- **Robo-Advisors and Online Brokerages:**
  - **Definition:** Robo-advisors and online brokerages often have fee structures that differ from traditional investment options.
  - **Significance:**
    - Understand the fee structure of these platforms, including management fees, transaction costs, and any other associated charges.

- **Tax Efficiency:**
  - **Definition:** Consider the tax efficiency of investment options, as taxes can impact overall returns.
  - **Significance:**
    - Passively managed index funds and ETFs often have lower turnover, leading to potential tax advantages compared to actively managed funds.

Environmental, Social, and Governance (ESG) considerations have become integral to socially responsible investing. When evaluating how well companies align with ethical and sustainability criteria, it's important to focus on key aspects within each category:

- **Environmental (E) Considerations:**
  - **Carbon Footprint:**
    - Assess a company's efforts to reduce greenhouse gas emissions and its overall carbon footprint.
    - Look for initiatives related to energy efficiency and the use of renewable energy sources.
  - **Resource Usage:**
    - Evaluate how efficiently a company utilizes natural resources and whether it has policies in place to minimize resource depletion.
  - **Waste Management:**
    - Consider a company's waste management practices and its commitment to reducing, recycling, or responsibly disposing of waste.
  - **Biodiversity Impact:**
    - Assess the impact of a company's operations on biodiversity and ecosystems, especially relevant for industries with potential environmental implications.
- **Social (S) Considerations:**
  - **Labor Practices:**
    - Evaluate how a company treats its employees, including fair wages, workplace safety, and adherence to labor laws.
    - Consider employee satisfaction, diversity and inclusion efforts, and training programs.
  - **Community Engagement:**
    - Assess a company's engagement with local communities, including philanthropy, community development projects, and initiatives that contribute positively to society.
  - **Human Rights:**

- - - Examine a company's commitment to upholding human rights in its operations and supply chain, avoiding involvement in any human rights abuses.
  - **Product Safety and Quality:**
    - Consider the safety and quality of a company's products or services, ensuring they meet ethical standards and do not pose risks to consumers.
- **Governance (G) Considerations:**
  - **Board Structure and Independence:**
    - Evaluate the composition of the company's board of directors, focusing on independence, diversity, and qualifications.
    - Assess whether there are mechanisms in place to prevent conflicts of interest.
  - **Executive Compensation:**
    - Examine the transparency and fairness of executive compensation structures.
    - Consider whether there are appropriate performance metrics tied to executive pay.
  - **Anti-Corruption Practices:**
    - Assess a company's commitment to combating corruption and bribery, including the implementation of anti-corruption policies.
  - **Shareholder Rights:**
    - Consider the protection of shareholder rights and whether the company encourages shareholder engagement.
    - Evaluate the mechanisms in place for shareholder voting and influence.
- **ESG Ratings and Frameworks:**
  - **Utilize ESG Ratings Agencies:**
    - Refer to ESG ratings agencies, such as MSCI, Sustainalytics, or others, which provide comprehensive assessments of companies based on ESG criteria.
  - **Global Reporting Initiative (GRI):**
    - Companies following the GRI standards provide detailed sustainability reports, offering insights into their environmental, social, and governance practices.
  - **Task Force on Climate-related Financial Disclosures (TCFD):**
    - Companies aligning with TCFD recommendations disclose climate-related risks and opportunities, providing transparency on climate-related financial impacts.
  - **UN Principles for Responsible Investment (PRI):**
    - Companies that adhere to the PRI principles commit to incorporating ESG factors into investment decision-making and ownership practices.
- **Industry-Specific Considerations:**
  - **Tailor ESG Criteria:**

- Recognize that ESG considerations can vary across industries. Tailor your assessment to industry-specific risks and opportunities.
- Industries with a higher environmental impact, such as energy or manufacturing, may face different ESG challenges than technology or healthcare sectors.

- **Future Sustainability Goals:**
  - **Look at Long-Term Commitments:**
    - Assess whether a company has set clear and achievable sustainability goals.
    - Companies with long-term commitments and transparent reporting demonstrate a commitment to ESG considerations.

By focusing on these aspects within the Environmental, Social, and Governance pillars, investors can make more informed decisions aligning with their values and contributing to sustainable and socially responsible investing.

Chapter 5: Monitoring and Adjusting Your Portfolio

Establishing Monitoring Mechanisms

Effective portfolio management doesn't end with the initial construction of your investment portfolio; continuous monitoring and adjustment are crucial to align the portfolio with changing market conditions and evolving financial goals. In this chapter, we explore the essential mechanisms for monitoring and adjusting your portfolio to ensure its ongoing relevance and performance.

1. Regular Portfolio Reviews:

- **Frequency:** Conduct periodic reviews of your portfolio at least quarterly or semi-annually.
- **Purpose:**
  - Evaluate the performance of each asset class and individual investments.

- Assess whether the portfolio remains aligned with your financial goals and risk tolerance.

2. Benchmark Comparison:

- **Select Appropriate Benchmarks:**
  - Choose benchmarks that represent the performance of the asset classes within your portfolio.
- **Regularly Compare:**
  - Regularly compare your portfolio's performance against the selected benchmarks.
  - Identify areas of overperformance or underperformance for further analysis.

3. Rebalancing Strategies:

- **Threshold-based Rebalancing:**
  - Set predefined percentage thresholds for each asset class. Trigger rebalancing when the actual allocation deviates significantly from the target.
- **Time-based Rebalancing:**
  - Rebalance the portfolio at predetermined intervals, such as quarterly or annually, regardless of the specific asset class percentages.
- **Tolerance Bands:**
  - Use tolerance bands to avoid unnecessary trading. Only rebalance when the allocation drifts beyond a certain range.

4. Economic and Market Analysis:

- **Stay Informed:**
  - Regularly analyze economic indicators, market trends, and geopolitical developments.
- **Adjust Based on Economic Conditions:**
  - Make strategic adjustments based on changing economic conditions and market outlook.

5. Review Financial Goals:

- **Regularly Assess Goals:**
  - Review your short-term and long-term financial goals regularly.
  - Adjust your portfolio to reflect changes in your financial circumstances or objectives.

6. Stay Updated on Tax Implications:

- **Understand Tax Consequences:**
  - Be aware of potential tax implications associated with portfolio changes.
- **Tax-Loss Harvesting:**
  - Consider tax-loss harvesting strategies to offset gains with losses and minimize tax liabilities.

7. Consider Life Changes:

- **Evaluate Life Events:**

- Assess the impact of significant life events, such as marriage, childbirth, or a career change, on your financial goals.
- **Adjust for Changing Circumstances:**
  - Adjust your portfolio to accommodate changes in income, expenses, or risk tolerance resulting from life events.

8. Monitor Fees and Expenses:

- **Regularly Review Fees:**
  - Periodically review the fees associated with your investments.
- **Explore Cost-Efficient Options:**
  - Explore cost-efficient investment options, especially if new, lower-cost alternatives become available.

9. Leverage Technology:

- **Use Portfolio Management Tools:**
  - Utilize online platforms and portfolio management tools to track and analyze your investments.
- **Automate Monitoring Processes:**
  - Automate alerts and notifications to stay informed about significant changes in your portfolio.

Assessing Investment Performance

1. Performance Metrics:

- **Total Return:** Evaluate the overall return of your portfolio, including capital gains and income.
- **Annualized Return:** Calculate the average annual return to assess performance over various time frames.
- **Risk-Adjusted Return:** Consider risk-adjusted metrics like the Sharpe ratio to assess returns relative to the level of risk taken.

2. Benchmark Comparison:

- **Select Appropriate Benchmarks:** Choose benchmarks that align with the asset classes in your portfolio.
- **Relative Performance:** Compare your portfolio's performance against the selected benchmarks to identify areas of strength or weakness.

3. Time-Weighted vs. Money-Weighted Returns:

- **Time-Weighted Returns:** Eliminate the impact of external cash flows to assess the performance of the investment strategy.
- **Money-Weighted Returns:** Incorporate the impact of cash flows, providing insights into the actual returns experienced by the investor.

4. Periodic Performance Reviews:

- **Regular Evaluations:** Conduct periodic reviews to assess how well your investments are meeting your financial goals.
- **Adjust Strategies:** Adjust your investment strategy based on the performance review to optimize for future outcomes.

Rebalancing Strategies

1. Threshold-Based Rebalancing:

- **Set Percentage Thresholds:** Define acceptable percentage deviations for each asset class.
- **Trigger Rebalancing:** Rebalance the portfolio when an asset class deviates beyond the established threshold.

2. Time-Based Rebalancing:

- **Regular Intervals:** Rebalance the portfolio at predetermined intervals (e.g., quarterly or annually).
- **Maintain Target Allocation:** Ensure the portfolio maintains its target asset allocation over time.

3. Tolerance Bands:

- **Define Tolerance Bands:** Establish upper and lower limits for each asset class.
- **Rebalance Within Bands:** Only rebalance when the actual allocation falls outside the defined tolerance bands.

4. Tax-Efficient Rebalancing:

- **Tax-Loss Harvesting:** Offset capital gains with capital losses to minimize tax implications.
- **Strategic Asset Location:** Place tax-efficient investments in taxable accounts and tax-inefficient ones in tax-advantaged accounts.

5. Portfolio Drift Monitoring:

- **Set Acceptable Drift Limits:** Define acceptable percentage drift limits for each asset class.
- **Regularly Monitor Drift:** Continuously monitor the portfolio for drift and rebalance when necessary.

Adapting to Changing Circumstances

1. Regular Financial Checkups:

- **Scheduled Assessments:** Conduct regular financial checkups to review your overall financial health.
- **Address Changes Promptly:** Address any changes in income, expenses, or financial goals promptly.

2. Life Event Adjustments:

- **Evaluate Impact:** Assess the impact of significant life events on your financial situation.
- **Adjust Portfolio Accordingly:** Make necessary adjustments to your portfolio to align with changing circumstances.

3. Periodic Risk Tolerance Reassessment:

- **Review Risk Tolerance:** Periodically reassess your risk tolerance based on changes in financial circumstances or personal preferences.
- **Adjust Asset Allocation:** Modify asset allocation to align with the reassessed risk tolerance.

4. Stay Informed About Market Conditions:

- **Monitor Economic Trends:** Stay informed about economic conditions, interest rates, and geopolitical events.
- **Adjust Strategy Accordingly:** Make strategic adjustments to your portfolio based on your analysis of changing market conditions.

5. Emergency Fund Management:

- **Ensure Adequate Emergency Fund:** Keep your emergency fund at an adequate level to handle unexpected expenses.
- **Avoid Overreliance on Investments:** Use investments primarily for long-term goals, ensuring short-term needs are covered separately.

6. Regular Communication with Advisors:

- **Consult with Financial Advisors:** Regularly communicate with financial advisors to discuss changes in circumstances or investment goals.
- **Leverage Professional Guidance:** Leverage the expertise of financial professionals to adapt your portfolio to changing financial landscapes.

Rebalancing is a crucial aspect of portfolio management that involves adjusting the asset allocation of your investment portfolio to bring it back in line with your target or desired allocation. This process ensures that your portfolio stays aligned with your investment goals and risk tolerance. Here are some common rebalancing strategies:

1. **Threshold-Based Rebalancing:**
   - **Set Percentage Thresholds:**
     - Define specific percentage thresholds for each asset class in your portfolio.
   - **Trigger Points:**
     - When an asset class deviates significantly from its target allocation (exceeds the threshold), trigger the rebalancing process.

2. **Time-Based Rebalancing:**
   - **Regular Intervals:**
     - Choose predefined time intervals for rebalancing, such as quarterly, semi-annually, or annually.
   - **Consistent Schedule:**
     - Regardless of market conditions, rebalance the portfolio at the scheduled intervals.

3. **Tolerance Bands:**
   - **Define Upper and Lower Bands:**
     - Set upper and lower percentage limits (tolerance bands) for each asset class.
   - **Rebalance Within Bands:**
     - Only initiate rebalancing when the actual allocation of an asset class falls outside the defined tolerance bands.

4. **Cash Flow Rebalancing:**
   - **Incorporate Cash Flows:**
     - Consider the impact of cash inflows (new investments) or outflows (withdrawals) on the overall asset allocation.
   - **Rebalance with Cash Flows:**
     - Use new contributions or withdrawals as opportunities to rebalance the portfolio.

5. **Volatility-Based Rebalancing:**
   - **Market Volatility Triggers:**
     - Implement rebalancing when market volatility surpasses a predefined threshold.
   - **Dynamic Adjustment:**

- Adjust the frequency of rebalancing based on the level of market volatility.

6. Tax-Efficient Rebalancing:
- **Tax-Loss Harvesting:**
  - Identify opportunities to offset capital gains with capital losses, minimizing tax implications.
- **Strategic Asset Location:**
  - Place tax-efficient investments in taxable accounts and tax-inefficient ones in tax-advantaged accounts.

7. Risk-Tolerance Rebalancing:
- **Periodic Risk Assessments:**
  - Reassess your risk tolerance periodically based on changes in financial circumstances or personal preferences.
- **Adjust Asset Allocation:**
  - Modify the asset allocation to align with the reassessed risk tolerance.

8. Portfolio Drift Monitoring:
- **Set Acceptable Drift Limits:**
  - Establish upper and lower percentage drift limits for each asset class.
- **Continuous Monitoring:**
  - Regularly monitor the actual allocation to detect and address any portfolio drift.

9. Strategic Rebalancing:
- **Market Conditions and Economic Trends:**
  - Consider broader market conditions and economic trends when rebalancing.
- **Adjust Strategy Accordingly:**
  - Make strategic adjustments to the portfolio based on your analysis of changing market conditions.

10. Dynamic Asset Allocation:
- **Flexible Asset Allocation:**
  - Adopt a dynamic approach that allows for flexibility in asset allocation based on market conditions.
- **Regular Review and Adjustments:**
  - Regularly review the investment landscape and adjust the portfolio as needed.

11. Ad Hoc Rebalancing:
- **Event-Driven Adjustments:**
  - Make rebalancing decisions based on significant events, such as changes in economic conditions or major shifts in market sentiment.
  - **Evaluate Market Opportunities:**
    - Take advantage of unique investment opportunities that arise unexpectedly.

Choosing the most appropriate rebalancing strategy depends on your specific financial goals, risk tolerance, and preferences. A combination of these strategies or a tailored approach based on your individual circumstances may provide the most effective way to maintain a well-balanced and resilient portfolio over time. Regularly reassess your strategy and make adjustments as needed to ensure your portfolio remains in line with your evolving financial objectives.

Real Case Scenario: Threshold-Based Rebalancing

Let's consider a hypothetical portfolio with the following target asset allocation:
- **Stocks:** 60%
- **Bonds:** 30%
- **Cash:** 10%

Thresholds for Rebalancing:
- **Stocks:** ±5%
- **Bonds:** ±3%
- **Cash:** ±2%

Initial Portfolio Allocation:
- **Stocks:** 62%
- **Bonds:** 28%
- **Cash:** 10%

Scenario:
- **Trigger Event:**
    - After a robust year for the stock market, the equity portion of the portfolio has increased to 62%, exceeding the 5% threshold.
- **Rebalancing Decision:**
    - The investor decides to initiate rebalancing to bring the stock allocation back to the target 60%.
- **Rebalancing Actions:**
    - Sell a portion of the stocks to reduce the allocation from 62% to 60%.
    - Use the proceeds to purchase bonds, increasing the bond allocation from 28% to 30%.
- **Post-Rebalancing Allocation:**
    - Stocks: 60%
    - Bonds: 30%
    - Cash: 10%

Impact:
- **Risk Management:**
    - By adhering to the threshold-based rebalancing strategy, the investor mitigates the risk associated with an overexposure to equities.
    - The portfolio is realigned with the original risk profile, reducing the potential impact of a market downturn on overall performance.
- **Discipline in Action:**
    - The rebalancing decision reflects the investor's discipline in adhering to a predefined strategy rather than being swayed by short-term market movements.
- **Continuous Monitoring:**
    - The investor continues to monitor market conditions and economic trends for potential future adjustments, ensuring the portfolio remains in line with long-term goals.

This real case scenario illustrates how a threshold-based rebalancing strategy works in practice.

Real Case Scenario: Time-Based Rebalancing

Let's explore a practical example of a time-based rebalancing strategy for a hypothetical portfolio with the following target allocation:

- **Stocks:** 60%

- **Bonds:** 30%
- **Cash:** 10%

Time-Based Rebalancing Schedule: Quarterly

Initial Portfolio Allocation (at the end of Quarter 1):
- **Stocks:** 58%
- **Bonds:** 32%
- **Cash:** 10%

Scenario:
- **Quarterly Review (End of Quarter 1):**
  - The investor reviews the portfolio at the end of the first quarter, comparing the current allocation to the target allocation.
- **Deviation from Target Allocation:**
  - Stocks have decreased to 58%, and bonds have increased to 32%, deviating slightly from the target allocation.
- **Rebalancing Decision:**
  - Following the time-based rebalancing schedule, the investor decides to bring the portfolio back to the target allocation.
- **Rebalancing Actions:**
  - Sell a portion of the bonds to reduce the allocation from 32% to 30%.
  - Use the proceeds to purchase stocks, increasing the stock allocation from 58% to 60%.
- **Post-Rebalancing Allocation:**
  - **Stocks:** 60%
  - **Bonds:** 30%
  - **Cash:** 10%

Impact:
- **Consistent Alignment:**
  - Time-based rebalancing ensures that the portfolio is consistently realigned with the target allocation, regardless of short-term market fluctuations.
- **Systematic Approach:**
  - The investor follows a systematic and disciplined approach, making adjustments at regular intervals to maintain the desired balance between asset classes.
- **Risk Mitigation:**
  - By rebalancing quarterly, the investor addresses potential drifts in the portfolio, mitigating the risk associated with overexposure to a particular asset class.
- **Long-Term Focus:**
  - The strategy reflects a long-term perspective, allowing the investor to navigate market cycles without making impulsive decisions based on short-term market movements.

This real case scenario illustrates how a time-based rebalancing strategy operates in practice. By adhering to a consistent schedule, the investor can systematically manage the portfolio's asset allocation over time, contributing to a more stable and goal-aligned investment approach.

Real Case Scenario: Tolerance Bands Rebalancing

Let's explore a practical example of a rebalancing strategy using tolerance bands for a hypothetical portfolio with the following target allocation:

- **Stocks:** 60%
- **Bonds:** 30%
- **Cash:** 10%

Tolerance Bands:

- **Stocks:** ±5%
- **Bonds:** ±3%
- **Cash:** ±2%

Initial Portfolio Allocation:
- **Stocks:** 62%
- **Bonds:** 28%
- **Cash:** 10%

Scenario:
- **Regular Portfolio Monitoring:**
    - The investor regularly monitors the portfolio allocation and identifies that the stock allocation has exceeded the upper tolerance band.
- **Deviation from Target Allocation:**
    - The stocks have increased to 62%, surpassing the upper limit of the 60% tolerance band.
- **Rebalancing Decision:**
    - In line with the tolerance bands strategy, the investor decides to rebalance the portfolio to bring the stock allocation back within the acceptable range.
- **Rebalancing Actions:**
    - Sell a portion of the stocks to reduce the allocation from 62% to 60%.
    - Use the proceeds to purchase bonds, increasing the bond allocation from 28% to 30%.
- **Post-Rebalancing Allocation:**
    - Stocks: 60%
    - Bonds: 30%
    - Cash: 10%

Impact:
- **Dynamic Adjustment:**
    - The investor employs a dynamic approach, allowing for flexibility within the specified tolerance bands to adapt to market movements.
- **Risk Management:**
    - Tolerance bands provide a systematic way to manage risk by establishing acceptable ranges for asset class allocations.
- **Discipline and Consistency:**
    - The investor demonstrates discipline by adhering to the predetermined tolerance bands, ensuring a consistent and controlled investment strategy.
- **Adaptability to Market Changes:**
    - Tolerance bands allow the portfolio to adapt to changing market conditions while maintaining a structured and goal-oriented investment approach.

Real Case Scenario: Cash Flow Rebalancing

Let's delve into a practical example of cash flow rebalancing for a hypothetical portfolio with the following target allocation:

- **Stocks:** 60%
- **Bonds:** 30%
- **Cash:** 10%

Initial Portfolio Allocation:

- **Stocks:** 58%
- **Bonds:** 32%
- **Cash:** 10%

Scenario:

- **Cash Inflow (New Investments):**
    - The investor receives a cash inflow, either through regular contributions to the portfolio or a lump-sum investment.
- **Impact on Asset Allocation:**

- - The new cash inflow increases the overall cash position in the portfolio.
- **Rebalancing Decision:**
  - The investor decides to use the cash inflow to rebalance the portfolio and bring it back to the target allocation.
- **Rebalancing Actions:**
  - Allocate a portion of the new cash to purchase additional stocks, increasing the stock allocation from 58% to 60%.
- **Post-Rebalancing Allocation:**
  - Stocks: 60%
  - Bonds: 30%
  - Cash: 10%

Impact:
- **Utilizing Cash Inflows:**
  - Cash flow rebalancing allows the investor to leverage incoming funds for strategic asset allocation adjustments.
- **Maintaining Target Allocation:**
  - By reallocating the cash to purchase stocks, the investor ensures that the portfolio maintains the desired target allocation.
- **Disciplined Approach:**
  - Cash flow rebalancing reflects a disciplined approach to managing the portfolio, actively using cash inflows to optimize asset allocation.
- **Adaptability to Market Changes:**
  - This strategy allows for adaptability, enabling the investor to respond to changing market conditions and capitalize on investment opportunities.

Conclusion:

Cash flow rebalancing provides a dynamic and efficient way to adjust the portfolio's asset allocation, especially in response to new contributions or inflows. By strategically deploying cash, investors can maintain discipline, align with their investment goals, and capitalize on market opportunities, contributing to a well-balanced and goal-oriented portfolio.

Real Case Scenario: Volatility-Based Rebalancing

Let's explore a practical example of a volatility-based rebalancing strategy for a hypothetical portfolio with the following target allocation:

- **Stocks:** 60%
- **Bonds:** 30%
- **Cash:** 10%

Volatility Threshold for Rebalancing: ±2%

Initial Portfolio Allocation:

- **Stocks:** 61%
- **Bonds:** 29%
- **Cash:** 10%

Scenario:

- **Monitoring Market Volatility:**
    - The investor regularly monitors market conditions and tracks the volatility of the stock market.
- **Volatility Threshold Exceeded:**
    - Due to increased market volatility, the volatility of stocks reaches the predetermined threshold of ±2%.
- **Rebalancing Decision:**

- In response to the elevated volatility, the investor decides to rebalance the portfolio to manage risk and maintain the desired allocation.
- **Rebalancing Actions:**
  - Sell a portion of the stocks to reduce the allocation from 61% to 60%.
  - Use the proceeds to purchase bonds, increasing the bond allocation from 29% to 30%.
- **Post-Rebalancing Allocation:**
  - **Stocks:** 60%
  - **Bonds:** 30%
  - **Cash:** 10%

Impact:
- **Risk Mitigation:**
  - Volatility-based rebalancing allows the investor to proactively manage risk by responding to increased market volatility.
- **Dynamic Asset Allocation:**
  - The strategy reflects a dynamic approach to asset allocation, adjusting the portfolio in response to changing market conditions.
- **Disciplined Execution:**
  - By adhering to a predefined volatility threshold, the investor demonstrates discipline in executing rebalancing decisions based on objective criteria.
- **Preserving Long-Term Goals:**
  - Volatility-based rebalancing aims to preserve the long-term goals of the portfolio by preventing excessive exposure to volatile asset classes.

Conclusion:
Volatility-based rebalancing provides a systematic approach to managing risk by adjusting the portfolio in response to changes in market volatility. This strategy allows investors to stay disciplined in the face of market fluctuations, ensuring that the portfolio remains aligned with their risk tolerance and long-term objectives. Regularly monitoring volatility and making adjustments accordingly contribute to a more resilient and goal-oriented investment approach.

Real Case Scenario: Tax-Efficient Rebalancing

Let's explore a practical example of tax-efficient rebalancing for a hypothetical portfolio with the following target allocation:

- **Stocks:** 60%
- **Bonds:** 30%
- **Cash:** 10%

Initial Portfolio Allocation:

- **Stocks:** 62%
- **Bonds:** 28%
- **Cash:** 10%

Scenario:

- **Capital Gains in Stocks:**
    - The stock portion of the portfolio has experienced significant capital gains, resulting in potential tax implications if sold.
- **Tax-Loss Harvesting Opportunity:**
    - Within the bond allocation, there are bonds that have experienced losses, providing an opportunity for tax-loss harvesting.
- **Rebalancing Decision:**
    - Instead of selling stocks with capital gains, the investor decides to harvest tax losses in bonds to rebalance the portfolio.
- **Rebalancing Actions:**
    - Sell bonds with losses to offset capital gains in stocks, maintaining the overall asset allocation.
    - Use the cash proceeds to purchase additional bonds to bring the bond allocation back to the target.
- **Post-Rebalancing Allocation:**
    - **Stocks:** 60%

        - Bonds: 30%
        - Cash: 10%

Impact:
- **Tax Efficiency:**
    - Tax-efficient rebalancing minimizes the tax impact by strategically harvesting losses, reducing the overall tax liability.
- **Preserving Capital Gains:**
    - The investor preserves capital gains in the stock portfolio by avoiding unnecessary sales, allowing the gains to compound over time.
- **Discipline and Tax Planning:**
    - The strategy demonstrates discipline in tax planning, utilizing tax-loss harvesting to rebalance without triggering additional tax liabilities.
- **Long-Term Wealth Preservation:**
    - By minimizing taxes and preserving capital gains, tax-efficient rebalancing contributes to the long-term wealth preservation goals of the portfolio.

Conclusion:
Tax-efficient rebalancing is a strategic approach that considers the tax implications of portfolio adjustments. This strategy aims to minimize taxes, preserve capital gains, and maintain a disciplined investment approach. By incorporating tax planning into the rebalancing process, investors can enhance the overall after-tax returns of their portfolios over the long term.

Real Case Scenario: Risk-Tolerance Rebalancing
Let's explore a practical example of risk-tolerance rebalancing for a hypothetical portfolio with the following target allocation:

- **Stocks:** 60%
- **Bonds:** 30%
- **Cash:** 10%

Risk Tolerance Assessment:

- The investor has a moderate risk tolerance but has recently experienced a decrease in risk tolerance due to changes in personal circumstances.

Initial Portfolio Allocation:
- **Stocks:** 62%
- **Bonds:** 28%
- **Cash:** 10%

Scenario:
- **Reassessment of Risk Tolerance:**
  - The investor undergoes a periodic review of their financial situation and personal circumstances.
- **Decreased Risk Tolerance:**
  - Due to changes such as approaching retirement or a significant life event, the investor's risk tolerance has decreased.
- **Rebalancing Decision:**
  - In response to the decreased risk tolerance, the investor decides to rebalance the portfolio to reduce exposure to equities.
- **Rebalancing Actions:**
  - Sell a portion of the stocks to reduce the allocation from 62% to 60%.
  - Allocate the proceeds to cash and bonds, increasing the bond allocation from 28% to 30%.
- **Post-Rebalancing Allocation:**
  - Stocks: 60%
  - Bonds: 30%
  - Cash: 10%

Impact:
- **Alignment with Risk Tolerance:**
  - Risk-tolerance rebalancing ensures that the portfolio aligns with the investor's current risk tolerance, providing a more comfortable investment experience.
- **Risk Mitigation:**
  - The strategy addresses the investor's desire for a more conservative approach, reducing exposure to potentially volatile asset classes.
- **Adapting to Life Changes:**
  - Risk-tolerance rebalancing demonstrates adaptability to life changes, recognizing the need to adjust the portfolio based on evolving circumstances.
- **Preserving Capital:**
  - By reducing exposure to higher-risk assets, the investor aims to preserve capital and minimize the impact of market volatility on the portfolio.

Conclusion:
Risk-tolerance rebalancing is essential for aligning the portfolio with an investor's comfort level with risk. This strategy allows individuals to adapt their investment approach based on changes in personal circumstances, ensuring that the portfolio remains well-suited to their risk tolerance and overall financial goals. Regular assessments and adjustments contribute to a more customized and resilient investment strategy.

Real Case Scenario: Portfolio Drift Monitoring

Let's explore a practical example of portfolio drift monitoring for a hypothetical portfolio with the following target allocation:

- **Stocks:** 60%
- **Bonds:** 30%
- **Cash:** 10%

Tolerance Bands for Drift:

- **Stocks:** ±3%
- **Bonds:** ±2%
- **Cash:** ±1%

Initial Portfolio Allocation:

- **Stocks:** 59%
- **Bonds:** 31%
- **Cash:** 10%

Scenario:

- **Regular Portfolio Monitoring:**
  - The investor consistently monitors the portfolio and notices that the actual allocation has drifted from the target allocation.
- **Drift Exceeds Tolerance Bands:**
  - The stock allocation has decreased to 59%, breaching the lower tolerance band of ±3%.
- **Rebalancing Decision:**
  - Recognizing the drift beyond the tolerance bands, the investor decides to rebalance the portfolio to bring it back within the acceptable range.
- **Rebalancing Actions:**
  - Sell a portion of bonds to reduce the bond allocation from 31% to 30%.
  - Allocate the proceeds to purchase additional stocks, increasing the stock allocation from 59% to 60%.
- **Post-Rebalancing Allocation:**
  - **Stocks:** 60%
  - **Bonds:** 30%
  - **Cash:** 10%

Impact:
- **Maintaining Disciplined Approach:**
  - Portfolio drift monitoring reflects the investor's commitment to maintaining a disciplined investment strategy aligned with the target allocation.
- **Mitigating Drift Effects:**
  - By promptly addressing drift beyond the tolerance bands, the investor mitigates the potential impact on overall portfolio risk and return.
- **Adapting to Market Movements:**
  - Portfolio drift monitoring ensures adaptability to market movements, allowing the investor to make strategic adjustments based on the evolving investment landscape.
- **Long-Term Goal Preservation:**
  - The investor aims to preserve the long-term goals of the portfolio by preventing significant deviations from the target allocation.

Conclusion:
Portfolio drift monitoring is a proactive strategy to ensure that the actual allocation of the portfolio remains within acceptable ranges. By regularly assessing the drift and taking corrective action, investors maintain a disciplined and goal-oriented investment approach. This approach contributes to the long-term success and resilience of the portfolio in the face of changing market conditions.

Real Case Scenario: Strategic Rebalancing

Let's explore a practical example of strategic rebalancing for a hypothetical portfolio with the following target allocation:

- **Stocks:** 60%
- **Bonds:** 30%
- **Cash:** 10%

Initial Portfolio Allocation:

- **Stocks:** 58%
- **Bonds:** 32%
- **Cash:** 10%

Scenario:
- **Assessment of Economic Conditions:**
  - The investor regularly monitors economic conditions, market trends, and geopolitical developments.
- **Changing Market Landscape:**
  - Based on a comprehensive analysis, the investor anticipates a shift in the market landscape, with potential opportunities and risks.
- **Rebalancing Decision:**
  - In response to the changing market outlook, the investor decides to strategically rebalance the portfolio to capitalize on emerging opportunities and mitigate potential risks.
- **Rebalancing Actions:**
  - Sell a portion of the bonds, as they are expected to underperform in the changing economic environment.
  - Allocate the proceeds to purchase additional stocks, anticipating growth opportunities in specific sectors.
- **Post-Rebalancing Allocation:**
  - **Stocks:** 60%
  - **Bonds:** 30%
  - **Cash:** 10%

Impact:
- **Strategic Asset Allocation:**
  - Strategic rebalancing reflects a proactive approach to asset allocation, aligning the portfolio with the investor's forward-looking market outlook.
- **Capitalizing on Opportunities:**
  - The investor takes advantage of perceived opportunities in the stock market, positioning the portfolio to benefit from anticipated growth.
- **Risk Management:**
  - By strategically reducing exposure to bonds, the investor mitigates potential risks associated with an economic environment less favorable to fixed-income securities.
- **Adaptability to Market Changes:**
  - Strategic rebalancing demonstrates the investor's adaptability to changing market conditions, emphasizing a forward-thinking and dynamic investment strategy.

Conclusion:
Strategic rebalancing involves making adjustments to the portfolio based on a comprehensive analysis of economic conditions and market trends. This proactive approach allows investors to capitalize on emerging opportunities, manage risks, and position their portfolios for potential market shifts. Strategic rebalancing is a valuable tool for investors who actively engage in market research and seek to optimize their portfolios based on a forward-looking investment strategy.

Real Case Scenario: Dynamic Asset Allocation

Let's explore a practical example of dynamic asset allocation for a hypothetical portfolio with the following target allocation:

- **Stocks:** 60%
- **Bonds:** 30%
- **Cash:** 10%

Initial Portfolio Allocation:

- **Stocks:** 62%
- **Bonds:** 28%
- **Cash:** 10%

Scenario:

- **Continuous Monitoring:**
  - The investor employs a dynamic asset allocation strategy, continuously monitoring market conditions, economic indicators, and geopolitical events.
- **Market Opportunities Identified:**
  - Through thorough analysis, the investor identifies an upcoming economic expansion that is likely to favor certain sectors, especially within the stock market.
- **Dynamic Rebalancing Decision:**
  - In response to the identified market opportunities, the investor decides to dynamically rebalance the portfolio to take advantage of the expected growth in specific sectors.
- **Rebalancing Actions:**
  - Sell a portion of the bonds and reallocate the funds to purchase stocks in sectors expected to outperform during the economic expansion.
- **Post-Rebalancing Allocation:**
  - **Stocks:** 65%
  - **Bonds:** 25%
  - **Cash:** 10%

Impact:
- **Adaptive Strategy:**
  - Dynamic asset allocation allows the investor to adapt the portfolio based on evolving market conditions, optimizing for potential opportunities.
- **Enhanced Returns:**
  - By strategically increasing exposure to sectors poised for growth, the investor aims to enhance the overall returns of the portfolio.
- **Risk Management:**
  - The dynamic approach includes a risk management component, ensuring the portfolio remains resilient to potential market downturns through diversified holdings.
- **Flexibility in Decision-Making:**
  - Dynamic asset allocation demonstrates the flexibility to make real-time decisions, responding to emerging trends and economic shifts.

Conclusion:
Dynamic asset allocation is a strategy that involves continuously monitoring and adjusting the portfolio based on changing market conditions. This approach allows investors to capitalize on opportunities, manage risks, and stay ahead of evolving economic trends. Dynamic asset allocation is well-suited for investors who actively engage in market research and prefer a flexible and adaptive investment strategy.

Real Case Scenario: Ad Hoc Rebalancing
Let's explore a practical example of ad hoc rebalancing for a hypothetical portfolio with the following target allocation:

- **Stocks:** 60%
- **Bonds:** 30%
- **Cash:** 10%

Initial Portfolio Allocation:

- **Stocks:** 62%
- **Bonds:** 28%
- **Cash:** 10%

Scenario:
- **Unexpected Market Event:**
  - The investor comes across unexpected market news that indicates a sudden and significant shift in the valuation of certain asset classes.
- **Ad Hoc Rebalancing Decision:**
  - Recognizing the potential impact of the unexpected event on the portfolio, the investor decides to initiate ad hoc rebalancing to safeguard against adverse consequences.
- **Rebalancing Actions:**
  - Sell a portion of the stocks in response to the market news.
  - Allocate the proceeds to increase the bond holdings, providing a defensive posture against potential market volatility.
- **Post-Rebalancing Allocation:**
  - Stocks: 58%
  - Bonds: 32%
  - Cash: 10%

Impact:
- **Reacting to Unforeseen Events:**
  - Ad hoc rebalancing allows the investor to promptly respond to unexpected market developments, providing a quick adjustment to the portfolio.
- **Risk Mitigation:**
  - The strategy aims to mitigate potential losses by reducing exposure to asset classes impacted by the unforeseen event.
- **Preserving Capital:**
  - By taking immediate action, the investor seeks to preserve capital and protect the portfolio from adverse market conditions.
- **Discipline in Decision-Making:**
  - Ad hoc rebalancing reflects the investor's ability to make disciplined decisions in response to real-time market events, showcasing adaptability and prudent risk management.

Conclusion:
Ad hoc rebalancing is a strategy that involves making spontaneous adjustments to the portfolio in response to unexpected market events. This approach allows investors to exercise flexibility and respond promptly to emerging risks or opportunities. While it may not follow a predefined schedule, ad hoc rebalancing is valuable in situations where immediate action is warranted to protect the portfolio from unforeseen market developments.

Chapter 5: Adapting to Changing Circumstances

In the dynamic world of finance, your personal circumstances, financial goals, and the overall economic landscape are subject to change. Adapting your investment strategy to these shifts is crucial for maintaining a robust and resilient portfolio. This chapter will guide you through the process of adapting to changing circumstances.

Establishing Monitoring Mechanisms

- **Regular Portfolio Check-ins:**
  - Set a routine for reviewing your portfolio's performance and assessing its alignment with your financial goals.
- **Financial Health Assessments:**
  - Periodically evaluate your overall financial health, considering changes in income, expenses, and other relevant factors.

Assessing Investment Performance

- **Performance Metrics:**
  - Utilize key performance indicators such as return on investment (ROI), risk-adjusted returns, and benchmark comparisons.
- **Goal Alignment:**
  - Ensure your portfolio's performance aligns with your short-term and long-term financial objectives.

Rebalancing Strategies

- **Flexible Rebalancing Schedule:**
  - Adopt a rebalancing schedule that allows for adjustments based on major life events, market conditions, or changes in risk tolerance.
- **Tax-Efficient Rebalancing:**
  - Consider tax implications when rebalancing, strategizing to minimize tax burdens during adjustments.

Adapting to Life Changes

- **Life Events Impact Analysis:**
  - Evaluate the impact of significant life events such as marriage, childbirth, or career changes on your financial goals and risk tolerance.

- **Portfolio Adjustments:**
  - Modify your portfolio to accommodate changes in priorities, time horizons, or income levels resulting from life events.

  Reallocation Based on Economic Trends
- **Market Research:**
  - Stay informed about broader economic trends, geopolitical events, and industry developments that may influence your investment strategy.
- **Strategic Shifts:**
  - Consider strategic reallocation based on economic forecasts, adjusting sector exposure and asset allocation accordingly.

  Continuous Learning and Financial Literacy
- **Stay Informed:**
  - Engage in ongoing education about financial markets, investment strategies, and emerging trends to make informed decisions.
- **Financial Advisor Consultations:**
  - Seek guidance from financial advisors to navigate complex financial situations and receive personalized advice.

  Embracing Flexibility
- **Open-Minded Approach:**
  - Maintain flexibility in your investment approach, being open to adjusting strategies based on evolving circumstances.
- **Dynamic Asset Allocation:**
  - Embrace dynamic asset allocation, allowing your portfolio to adapt to changing market conditions and economic environments.

  Adapting to changing circumstances is an integral part of successful portfolio management. By establishing monitoring mechanisms, regularly assessing performance, and remaining open to adjustments, you can navigate the complexities of the financial landscape with confidence and resilience.

Chapter 6: Tax Efficiency and Portfolio Management

Efficiently managing taxes is a crucial aspect of optimizing investment returns and preserving wealth. This chapter delves into the intricate relationship between taxes and portfolio management, offering strategies to minimize tax liabilities while maximizing after-tax returns.

Understanding Tax Implications

- **Taxable Events:**
  - Identify common taxable events such as capital gains, dividends, and interest income that impact your investment returns.
- **Tax Bracket Considerations:**
  - Assess your current tax bracket to make informed decisions about realizing gains or losses.

Tax-Efficient Investment Vehicles

- **Tax-Advantaged Accounts:**
  - Leverage tax-advantaged accounts such as 401(k)s, IRAs, and 529 plans to benefit from tax deferral or exemptions.
- **Asset Location Strategies:**
  - Strategically allocate assets across taxable and tax-advantaged accounts to optimize tax efficiency.

Tax-Loss Harvesting

- **Identifying Losses:**
  - Actively monitor your portfolio for investments in a loss position that can be strategically sold to offset gains.
- **Timing Considerations:**
  - Implement tax-loss harvesting opportunistically, considering market conditions and future capital gains.

Dividend and Interest Income Strategies

- **Dividend Reinvestment Plans (DRIPs):**
  - Consider using DRIPs to automatically reinvest dividends, potentially reducing tax implications.
- **Tax-Efficient Bond Investments:**
  - Explore tax-efficient bond options, such as municipal bonds, to minimize tax on interest income.

Managing Capital Gains

- **Long-Term vs. Short-Term Gains:**
  - Understand the tax implications of long-term and short-term capital gains and adjust your investment strategy accordingly.
- **Tax-Loss Harvesting for Offsetting Gains:**
  - Utilize tax-loss harvesting to offset capital gains, mitigating the overall tax impact.

Minimizing Turnover
- **Impact of High Turnover:**
  - Recognize the potential tax consequences of frequent trading and high portfolio turnover.
- **Strategic Trading:**
  - Implement a strategic trading approach to minimize turnover and associated tax liabilities.

Tax-Efficient Withdrawal Strategies
- **Strategic Withdrawals:**
  - Plan withdrawals from tax-advantaged accounts strategically to optimize tax efficiency during retirement.
- **Roth IRA Conversion Considerations:**
  - Evaluate the potential benefits of Roth IRA conversions for tax diversification in retirement.

Working with Tax Professionals
- **Collaborating with Tax Advisors:**
  - Seek guidance from tax professionals to navigate complex tax regulations and tailor your investment strategy to your specific tax situation.
- **Staying Informed about Tax Laws:**
  - Stay abreast of changes in tax laws and regulations to make proactive adjustments to your investment strategy.

Tax-Efficient Charitable Giving
- **Donor-Advised Funds:**
  - Utilize donor-advised funds for tax-efficient charitable giving, allowing for strategic donation planning.
- **Appreciated Securities Donations:**
  - Consider donating appreciated securities to charities to minimize capital gains taxes.

Regular Portfolio Tax Reviews
- **Annual Tax Review:**
  - Conduct an annual review of your portfolio's tax implications and adjust your strategy as needed.
- **Tax-Efficient Rebalancing:**
  - Integrate tax efficiency into your rebalancing strategy, aiming to minimize tax consequences.

Understanding Tax Implications

Navigating the complexities of taxes is fundamental to effective portfolio management. Recognizing how different investment activities impact your tax liability is crucial for making informed decisions. In this section, we explore key considerations for understanding tax implications:

1. **Taxable Events:**
    - **Definition:** Taxable events are transactions that trigger a tax consequence.
    - **Examples:** Selling securities, receiving dividends, and earning interest income are common taxable events.
    - **Impact:** Different events may result in capital gains, ordinary income, or tax deductions, affecting your overall tax liability.
2. **Tax Bracket Considerations:**
    - **Definition:** Tax brackets determine the rate at which your income is taxed.
    - **Effect on Investments:** Assess your current tax bracket to determine the tax rate applied to your investment gains or losses.
    - **Strategic Decisions:** Understanding your tax bracket can influence decisions on realizing gains or losses based on your unique tax situation.
3. **Timing of Capital Gains:**
    - **Definition:** Capital gains can be categorized as short-term or long-term based on the holding period.
    - **Tax Rates:** Short-term gains are taxed at higher rates than long-term gains.
    - **Strategies:** Consider holding investments for the long term to benefit from lower tax rates on capital gains.
4. **Dividends and Interest Income:**
    - **Dividend Taxation:** Dividends may be subject to different tax rates, including qualified dividend rates.
    - **Interest Income:** Interest income is generally taxed at ordinary income rates.
    - **Strategies:** Utilize tax-efficient investments or accounts to manage the impact of dividend and interest income on your taxes.
5. **Tax-Loss Harvesting:**
    - **Definition:** Tax-loss harvesting involves selling investments at a loss to offset capital gains.
    - **Strategic Use:** Implement tax-loss harvesting to reduce tax liabilities during years with capital gains.
    - **Caution:** Be mindful of wash-sale rules that limit repurchasing the same security within a specific timeframe.
6. **Tax-Efficient Investment Vehicles:**
    - **Tax-Advantaged Accounts:** Accounts like IRAs and 401(k)s offer tax advantages, including tax deferral or tax-free withdrawals.
    - **Asset Location Strategies:** Allocate assets strategically across taxable and tax-advantaged accounts to optimize tax efficiency.

7. **Capital Gains Distributions:**
   - **Mutual Fund Considerations:** Mutual funds may distribute capital gains to shareholders.
   - **Tax Impact:** Understand the tax consequences of capital gains distributions and evaluate their impact on your overall tax situation.
8. **Tax Planning for Charitable Giving:**
   - **Donor-Advised Funds:** Utilize donor-advised funds for strategic charitable giving, allowing for potential tax deductions.
   - **Appreciated Securities Donations:** Donate appreciated securities to charities to minimize capital gains taxes.
9. **Consulting Tax Professionals:**
   - **Expert Guidance:** Work with tax professionals to navigate complex tax regulations and receive personalized advice.
   - **Annual Reviews:** Conduct regular reviews with tax advisors to align your investment strategy with current tax laws and regulations.

Tax-Efficient Investment Strategies

Effective tax planning is integral to optimizing investment returns. Implementing tax-efficient investment strategies can help minimize tax liabilities and enhance after-tax returns. In this section, we explore key strategies to make your investment approach more tax-efficient:

1. **Tax-Advantaged Accounts:**
   - **Utilize Retirement Accounts:** Contribute to tax-advantaged accounts such as 401(k)s, IRAs, and Roth IRAs to benefit from tax deferral or tax-free withdrawals.
   - **Strategic Contributions:** Make contributions based on your current and future tax situation, considering factors like tax brackets.
2. **Asset Location Strategies:**
   - **Strategically Allocate Assets:** Distribute assets across taxable and tax-advantaged accounts to optimize tax efficiency.
   - **Tax-inefficient Assets in Tax-Advantaged Accounts:** Hold tax-inefficient assets, such as bonds with interest income, in tax-advantaged accounts.
3. **Tax-Loss Harvesting:**
   - **Proactive Loss Management:** Implement tax-loss harvesting by selling investments at a loss to offset capital gains.
   - **Strategic Timing:** Harvest losses strategically, considering market conditions and the potential impact on your overall tax situation.
4. **Dividend Reinvestment Plans (DRIPs):**
   - **Automatic Reinvestment:** Enroll in DRIPs to automatically reinvest dividends, potentially reducing tax implications.
   - **Considerations:** Evaluate the tax consequences and eligibility for preferential tax rates on qualified dividends.

5. **Tax-Efficient Bond Investments:**
   - **Explore Municipal Bonds:** Consider tax-efficient bond options, such as municipal bonds, which may provide tax-free interest income.
   - **Tax-Advantaged Accounts for Bonds:** Allocate taxable bonds to tax-advantaged accounts to minimize tax on interest income.
6. **Capital Gains Planning:**
   - **Long-Term Holding:** Favor long-term holding of investments to benefit from lower tax rates on capital gains.
   - **Strategic Realization:** Consider realizing capital gains strategically, aligning with your tax situation and overall financial goals.
7. **Minimize Portfolio Turnover:**
   - **Impact of High Turnover:** Recognize the tax consequences of frequent trading and high portfolio turnover.
   - **Strategic Trading:** Implement a strategic trading approach to minimize turnover and associated tax liabilities.
8. **Tax-Efficient Withdrawal Strategies:**
   - **Withdrawal Timing:** Strategically plan withdrawals from tax-advantaged accounts to optimize tax efficiency during retirement.
   - **Roth IRA Conversions:** Evaluate the benefits of Roth IRA conversions for tax diversification and potentially tax-free withdrawals.
9. **Tax-Efficient Charitable Giving:**
   - **Donor-Advised Funds:** Utilize donor-advised funds for tax-efficient charitable giving, allowing for strategic donation planning.
   - **Appreciated Securities Donations:** Donate appreciated securities to charities to minimize capital gains taxes.
10. **Tax-Efficient Investments:**
    - **Tax-Efficient Funds:** Invest in tax-efficient mutual funds or exchange-traded funds (ETFs) that are designed to minimize taxable distributions.
    - **Strategic Asset Selection:** Choose tax-efficient investments that align with your overall portfolio strategy.
11. **Stay Informed about Tax Laws:**
    - **Regular Updates:** Stay abreast of changes in tax laws and regulations that may impact your investment strategy.
    - **Consult with Tax Professionals:** Regularly consult with tax professionals to ensure your strategy aligns with the current tax landscape.
12. **Tax Planning for Estate Management:**
    - **Estate Tax Considerations:** Consider estate planning strategies to minimize tax implications for heirs and beneficiaries.
    - **Gifting Strategies:** Explore tax-efficient gifting strategies to transfer wealth while minimizing potential estate taxes.

Chapter 7: Reinvesting and Compounding

Reinvesting and harnessing the power of compounding are essential elements of long-term wealth accumulation. This chapter explores the strategies and benefits of reinvestment and compounding, guiding you on maximizing the growth potential of your investments.

1. The Power of Compounding:
- **Definition:** Understand the concept of compounding, where the returns on your investments generate additional earnings over time.
- **Time Horizon Significance:** Recognize the significance of time in compounding, emphasizing the longer your money is invested, the more it can grow.

2. Reinvesting Dividends and Interest:
- **Automatic Reinvestment Plans:** Explore the benefits of automatic dividend reinvestment plans (DRIPs) to reinvest dividends and compound returns.
- **Interest Income Reinvestment:** Consider reinvesting interest income, especially in tax-advantaged accounts, to compound growth.

3. Compound Interest and Long-Term Growth:
- **Continuous Reinvestment:** Emphasize the impact of consistent reinvestment on the exponential growth of investments.
- **Strategic Contributions:** Regularly contribute additional funds to maximize the compounding effect over the long term.

4. Reinvesting Capital Gains:
- **Strategic Capital Gains Reinvestment:** Consider reinvesting realized capital gains strategically to capitalize on compounding.
- **Tax Considerations:** Be mindful of tax implications when reinvesting capital gains, balancing the benefits of compounding with tax efficiency.

5. Compounding in Tax-Advantaged Accounts:
- **Tax-Deferred Growth:** Leverage the tax-deferred growth within accounts like IRAs and 401(k)s to enhance the compounding effect.
- **Roth IRA Benefits:** Understand the tax-free growth potential of Roth IRAs and the compounding advantages they offer.

6. Dollar-Cost Averaging for Consistent Investment:
- **Steady Contributions:** Adopt a dollar-cost averaging strategy by making consistent contributions, taking advantage of market fluctuations.
- **Mitigating Market Timing Risks:** Use dollar-cost averaging to reduce the impact of market timing on your overall investment returns.

7. Reinvestment in Diversified Assets:
- **Diversify Reinvestments:** Reinvest in a diversified portfolio of assets to spread risk and capture growth opportunities across various sectors.
- **Strategic Asset Allocation:** Align reinvestment decisions with your overall asset allocation strategy for balanced growth.

8. Reinvesting in Dividend Growth Stocks:
- **Dividend Reinvestment for Stock Acquisition:** Reinvest dividends, particularly from dividend growth stocks, to acquire additional shares and compound wealth.
- **Long-Term Income Growth:** Benefit from the compounding effect of increasing dividend payouts over time.

9. The Impact of Reinvestment on Retirement Planning:
- **Retirement Savings Growth:** Visualize the impact of continuous reinvestment on the growth of your retirement savings.
- **Long-Term Wealth Accumulation:** Understand how compounding can contribute significantly to building a robust retirement nest egg.

10. Automating Reinvestment Strategies:
- **Set Up Automatic Reinvestment:** Streamline the compounding process by automating reinvestment strategies through brokerage settings.
- **Consistent and Disciplined Approach:** Ensure a consistent and disciplined approach to reinvestment by utilizing automation.

11. Periodic Review and Adjustment:
- **Review Investment Goals:** Periodically review your investment goals and adjust your reinvestment strategy to align with changing financial objectives.
- **Optimize Portfolio Composition:** Assess the performance of your portfolio and make necessary adjustments to optimize the composition for compounding growth.

12. Realizing the Long-Term Benefits:
- **Patience and Persistence:** Acknowledge that compounding is a long-term process, requiring patience and persistence for maximum effectiveness.
- **Weathering Market Volatility:** Be prepared to withstand market fluctuations and stay committed to your compounding strategy through various market conditions.

Conclusion: Unlocking the Potential of Reinvestment and Compounding:
- **Strategic Implementation:** Summarize the importance of strategically reinvesting dividends, interest, and capital gains to harness the power of compounding.
- **Long-Term Wealth Building:** Reinforce the concept that consistent and disciplined reinvestment is a cornerstone of long-term wealth accumulation.

Reinvesting and compounding form the bedrock of wealth accumulation strategies. By understanding and implementing these principles, investors can unlock the full potential of their investments, allowing their wealth to grow exponentially over time. This chapter provides actionable insights to guide readers in developing effective reinvestment strategies and harnessing the profound impact of compounding on their financial journey.

The Power of Compounding: Unleashing Exponential Growth

The concept of compounding is a financial phenomenon that has been aptly described as one of the most powerful forces in the universe. At its essence, compounding refers to the process where the returns on an investment generate additional earnings, and these earnings, in turn, generate more earnings. This compounding effect has a profound impact on the growth of wealth over time.

1. Understanding Compounding:
- **Exponential Growth:** Compounding doesn't operate in a linear fashion; instead, it leads to exponential growth. The longer the money is allowed to compound, the more significant its impact becomes.
- **Principal and Earnings:** Initially, compounding involves the reinvestment of both the original principal amount and the accumulated earnings. Over time, the earnings on the reinvested amounts contribute substantially to overall returns.

2. Time as the Key Factor:
- **The Time Horizon Significance:** The key factor driving the power of compounding is time. The more time an investment has to compound, the more wealth it can generate.
- **Patience Pays Off:** Compounding rewards patience. Even modest returns can lead to substantial wealth accumulation when given enough time to compound.

3. Compounding in Action:
- **Example Scenario:** Consider an investment of $10,000 with an annual return of 8%. In the first year, you earn $800 in interest. In the second year, your return is not just on the initial $10,000 but on $10,800, leading to a higher return.
- **Continuous Growth:** As this process continues over several years, the earnings contribute to an ever-growing base, resulting in a snowball effect.

4. Reinvesting for Maximum Impact:
- **Automatic Reinvestment:** Reinvesting dividends, interest, and any capital gains allows for continuous compounding. This is why strategies like automatic dividend reinvestment plans (DRIPs) are powerful.
- **Consistent Contributions:** Making regular contributions to an investment further fuels the compounding effect, creating a compounding cycle of both time and additional funds.

5. Compound Interest vs. Simple Interest:
- **Simple vs. Compound Interest:** In a simple interest scenario, earnings are calculated only on the initial principal. In a compound interest scenario, earnings are calculated on both the initial principal and the accumulated interest.
- **Growth Differential:** Over time, the growth differential between simple and compound interest becomes substantial.

6. Real-Life Implications:
- **Long-Term Wealth Accumulation:** Compounding is a critical factor in long-term wealth accumulation, making it an indispensable tool for retirement planning, education funds, and generational wealth building.
- **Mitigating Market Volatility:** The compounding effect helps smooth out the impact of market volatility over an extended period. Short-term market fluctuations have less impact on the overall trajectory of a well-compounded portfolio.

7. Harnessing Compounding for Financial Success:
- **Start Early:** The earlier you start investing, the more time your money has to compound. Starting early allows even modest amounts to grow into substantial wealth.
- **Consistent and Disciplined Approach:** A consistent and disciplined approach to investing, coupled with regular contributions and reinvestment, maximizes the benefits of compounding.

Conclusion: The Timeless Power of Compounding:
In conclusion, the power of compounding is timeless and universal. Whether you are just starting your investment journey or are a seasoned investor, understanding and leveraging the force of compounding is fundamental to financial success. Patience, a long-term perspective, and strategic reinvestment are the keys to unlocking the full potential of compounding, ensuring a journey of sustained and exponential wealth growth over time.

Reinvesting Dividends and Interest: Accelerating Wealth Growth
Reinvesting dividends and interest is a strategic approach that can significantly enhance the growth of your investment portfolio over time. This process capitalizes on the power of compounding, allowing your earnings to generate additional earnings. Let's delve into the nuances of reinvesting dividends and interest to better understand how it can accelerate the growth of your wealth.

1. Automatic Reinvestment Plans (DRIPs):
- **Definition:** Automatic Dividend Reinvestment Plans (DRIPs) are programs offered by many companies and investment platforms that enable investors to automatically reinvest their cash dividends to purchase additional shares of the same stock or fund.

- **Mechanism:** Instead of receiving dividends in cash, DRIPs use the dividends to buy more shares at the current market price, facilitating a seamless and continuous reinvestment process.

2. Benefits of Reinvesting Dividends:

- **Compounding Effect:** Reinvesting dividends ensures that not only your initial investment but also the dividends generated are earning returns. This compounds the growth of your investment over time.
- **Dollar-Cost Averaging:** DRIPs embrace the principle of dollar-cost averaging, where investors buy more shares when prices are low and fewer shares when prices are high. This strategy helps mitigate the impact of market volatility.

3. Tax Considerations for Dividend Reinvestment:

- **Tax Efficiency:** Reinvesting dividends within tax-advantaged accounts, such as IRAs or 401(k)s, can enhance tax efficiency. Since dividends are automatically reinvested, you may avoid immediate tax consequences.
- **Taxable Accounts:** In taxable accounts, reinvested dividends are still subject to taxes. Consider the potential tax implications when deciding whether to reinvest dividends or receive them as cash.

4. Interest Income Reinvestment:

- **Interest from Bonds or Savings Accounts:** Reinvesting interest income, especially from bonds or savings accounts, involves using the earned interest to purchase additional bonds or securities.
- **Compound Growth:** Similar to dividend reinvestment, reinvesting interest compounds the growth of the investment by earning returns on the original principal and the reinvested interest.

5. The Compounding Effect of Interest Reinvestment:

- **Continuous Earnings:** As interest is reinvested, it continues to generate more interest in subsequent periods. This compounding effect ensures that the growth of the investment becomes exponential.
- **Long-Term Wealth Accumulation:** Over a more extended period, the compounding effect of reinvested interest can significantly contribute to long-term wealth accumulation.

6. Considerations for Reinvestment Strategies:

- **Strategic Asset Allocation:** When reinvesting dividends and interest, align the strategy with your overall asset allocation. Ensure that the reinvestments complement your investment goals and risk tolerance.
- **Portfolio Diversification:** Reinvest in a diversified portfolio of assets to spread risk and capture growth opportunities across various sectors.

7. Setting Up Automatic Reinvestment:

- **Brokerage Settings:** Most brokerage platforms offer options to set up automatic dividend and interest reinvestment. Take advantage of these settings to streamline the process.
- **Consistency and Discipline:** Automation fosters consistency and discipline in your investment approach, ensuring that reinvestment occurs systematically.

8. Reinvesting for Retirement Planning:
- **Long-Term Wealth Growth:** Reinvesting dividends and interest is particularly powerful in retirement planning. The compounding effect over the course of a career can contribute significantly to retirement savings.
- **Creating a Sustainable Income Stream:** Continuously reinvesting dividends and interest can help create a sustainable income stream during retirement, especially when invested in income-generating assets.

Conclusion: Harnessing the Growth Potential:
Reinvesting dividends and interest is a dynamic strategy that harnesses the growth potential of compounding. By automatically reinvesting these earnings, investors create a continuous cycle of growth that can significantly accelerate wealth accumulation over time. Whether aiming for long-term wealth growth or building a sustainable income stream for retirement, the strategic and disciplined approach of reinvesting dividends and interest lays the foundation for financial success.

Long-Term Growth Strategies: Building Wealth with Patience and Strategy
Long-term growth strategies are instrumental in achieving sustained financial success, especially when it comes to building wealth and securing your financial future. These strategies involve a disciplined and patient approach to investing, capitalizing on the power of compounding and strategic decision-making. Let's delve deeper into the key components and principles of long-term growth strategies.

1. Strategic Asset Allocation:
- **Diversification:** Allocate your investments across a diversified mix of asset classes such as stocks, bonds, and real estate. Diversification helps mitigate risk and enhances the potential for stable, long-term growth.
- **Risk Tolerance:** Align your asset allocation with your risk tolerance and investment goals. While stocks may offer higher returns, they also come with higher volatility. Striking the right balance is crucial for long-term success.

2. Quality Stock Investments:
- **Focus on Fundamentals:** Choose stocks based on strong fundamentals, including earnings growth, low debt levels, and a history of consistent performance. Quality stocks have the potential for sustained growth over the long term.

- **Dividend Growth Stocks:** Consider investing in dividend growth stocks. Companies that consistently increase their dividends often exhibit financial stability and have the potential for both income and capital appreciation.

3. Consistent Contributions and Dollar-Cost Averaging:
- **Regular Contributions:** Make consistent contributions to your investment portfolio, especially in tax-advantaged accounts like IRAs and 401(k)s. Regular contributions, regardless of market conditions, capitalize on the power of dollar-cost averaging.
- **Mitigating Market Timing Risks:** Dollar-cost averaging involves buying more shares when prices are low and fewer shares when prices are high. This strategy helps mitigate the risks associated with trying to time the market.

4. Reinvesting Dividends and Interest:
- **Automatic Reinvestment Plans:** Leverage automatic reinvestment plans (DRIPs) to reinvest dividends and interest. This strategy ensures that earnings are continuously working to generate additional returns, compounding growth over time.
- **Enhancing Compound Growth:** Reinvesting dividends and interest is a powerful way to enhance the compounding effect. The longer these earnings are reinvested, the more significant their impact on long-term wealth accumulation.

5. Tax-Efficient Strategies:
- **Tax-Advantaged Accounts:** Maximize contributions to tax-advantaged accounts like IRAs and 401(k)s. These accounts offer tax benefits, including tax deferral or, in the case of Roth IRAs, tax-free withdrawals in retirement.
- **Tax-Loss Harvesting:** Implement tax-loss harvesting strategies to offset capital gains and minimize tax liabilities. This can enhance after-tax returns and contribute to long-term growth.

6. Patience and Discipline:
- **Long-Term Perspective:** Adopt a long-term perspective and resist the urge to react to short-term market fluctuations. Patience is a key virtue when pursuing sustained, compounding growth.
- **Disciplined Investing:** Stick to your investment strategy and resist making impulsive decisions based on market noise. A disciplined approach involves staying true to your long-term goals and strategies.

7. Review and Adjust:
- **Periodic Portfolio Reviews:** Conduct regular reviews of your investment portfolio to ensure it aligns with your long-term goals. Rebalance the portfolio as needed to maintain the desired asset allocation.
- **Adjust Based on Life Changes:** Life circumstances may change, impacting your financial goals. Adjust your long-term growth strategy accordingly, considering factors such as career changes, family events, or economic shifts.

8. Educate Yourself and Stay Informed:
- **Continuous Learning:** Stay informed about market trends, economic indicators, and investment strategies. Continuous learning empowers you to make informed decisions and adapt to evolving financial landscapes.

- **Financial Literacy:** Enhance your financial literacy to make sound investment choices. Understanding the fundamentals of investing equips you to navigate the complexities of the financial markets with confidence.

Conclusion: Building Generational Wealth:

Long-term growth strategies are the bedrock of building generational wealth. By combining strategic asset allocation, quality stock investments, consistent contributions, and tax-efficient practices with patience and discipline, investors can pave the way for sustained financial success. The compounding effect, when harnessed through these strategies, transforms investments into a powerful vehicle for building wealth over the long term.

Chapter 8: Navigating Economic Challenges

In the dynamic landscape of personal finance, individuals often encounter various economic challenges that can impact their financial well-being. This chapter explores strategies and insights to navigate economic challenges effectively, ensuring resilience and financial stability in the face of uncertainties.

1. Economic Downturns and Job Loss:
- **Emergency Fund Importance:** Emphasize the significance of maintaining an emergency fund to cover living expenses in case of job loss or economic downturns.
- **Debt Management:** Discuss prudent debt management strategies to alleviate financial strain during challenging economic periods.
- **Networking and Skill Enhancement:** Encourage continuous networking and skill enhancement to enhance employability during economic uncertainties.

2. Inflation and Purchasing Power:
- **Investment Diversification:** Highlight the role of diversified investments, including inflation-resistant assets like real estate and commodities, in preserving purchasing power.
- **Adjustment of Budgets:** Advise on periodically adjusting budgets to account for potential increases in living costs due to inflation.
- **Investing in TIPS:** Consider Treasury Inflation-Protected Securities (TIPS) as an option for protecting investments against inflation.

3. Market Volatility and Investment Strategies:
- **Long-Term Investment Perspective:** Reinforce the importance of maintaining a long-term investment perspective amidst market fluctuations.
- **Dollar-Cost Averaging:** Advocate for the use of dollar-cost averaging to mitigate the impact of market volatility on investment portfolios.
- **Rebalancing Strategies:** Discuss strategic portfolio rebalancing to align investments with long-term goals during market turbulence.

4. Rising Interest Rates:
- **Impact on Borrowing Costs:** Explain how rising interest rates can affect borrowing costs and encourage responsible debt management.

- **Adjustment of Investment Portfolios:** Discuss potential adjustments to investment portfolios, considering the impact of rising rates on different asset classes.
- **Consideration for Fixed-Income Investments:** Evaluate the impact on fixed-income investments and explore alternatives such as floating-rate bonds.

5. **Currency Fluctuations and Global Investments:**
   - **Diversification Benefits:** Illustrate how global diversification can mitigate risks associated with currency fluctuations.
   - **Hedging Strategies:** Discuss hedging strategies for international investments to manage exposure to currency risk.
   - **Understanding Currency Impacts:** Enhance understanding of how currency movements can affect the value of international investments.

6. **Healthcare Costs and Insurance Planning:**
   - **Importance of Health Insurance:** Stress the critical role of health insurance in protecting against unexpected healthcare expenses.
   - **Health Savings Accounts (HSAs):** Explore the benefits of HSAs as a tool for tax-advantaged healthcare savings.
   - **Regular Health Checkups:** Encourage proactive healthcare measures to prevent and detect health issues early, minimizing potential financial impact.

7. **Housing Market Instabilities:**
   - **Evaluate Housing Investments:** Advise on thoughtful consideration before making significant housing investments during periods of market instability.
   - **Emergency Housing Fund:** Suggest the establishment of an emergency housing fund to address unforeseen housing-related challenges.
   - **Rental Market Considerations:** Discuss the option of renting versus buying during uncertain housing market conditions.

8. **Technological Disruptions and Career Adaptability:**
   - **Continuous Learning:** Promote a culture of continuous learning to adapt to technological changes and stay relevant in evolving industries.
   - **Diversification of Skills:** Encourage the development of a diverse skill set to enhance career adaptability.
   - **Technology as an Asset:** Highlight the potential of leveraging technology for career growth and income diversification.

9. **Government Policies and Fiscal Planning:**
   - **Understanding Policy Impacts:** Foster an understanding of how government policies can influence personal finances.
   - **Tax Planning:** Advocate for proactive tax planning to optimize financial outcomes based on evolving fiscal policies.
   - **Public Assistance Programs:** Inform about available public assistance programs during economic challenges and how to access them when needed.

10. **Psychological Resilience and Mental Well-being:**
    - **Stress Management:** Acknowledge the psychological impact of economic challenges and emphasize the importance of stress management.

- **Seeking Professional Support:** Encourage seeking professional mental health support when navigating financial stress.
- **Community Resources:** Provide information on community resources and support networks available during challenging times.

Conclusion: Building Financial Resilience:
- **Holistic Approach:** Summarize the importance of a holistic approach to financial planning that considers economic challenges from various angles.
- **Adaptability and Preparedness:** Reinforce the value of adaptability, preparedness, and continuous learning in building financial resilience.
- **Community and Support Systems:** Emphasize the role of community and support systems in overcoming economic challenges and fostering overall well-being.

Navigating economic challenges requires a multifaceted and adaptive approach. By proactively addressing potential issues and building resilience, individuals can better weather uncertainties and maintain financial stability over the long term. This chapter serves as a guide to empower readers in navigating economic challenges with confidence and strategic planning.

Staying Focused on Long-Term Goals: Navigating Short-Term Distractions
In the pursuit of long-term financial success, staying focused on your goals is paramount, even in the face of short-term distractions and challenges. This chapter delves into strategies and mindset shifts that empower individuals to maintain unwavering focus on their long-term financial objectives.

1. Clarity of Long-Term Goals:
- **Define and Prioritize Goals:** Begin by clearly defining your long-term financial goals. Prioritize them based on importance and alignment with your life aspirations.
- **Visualization Techniques:** Utilize visualization techniques to create a vivid mental image of achieving your long-term goals. This enhances motivation and helps overcome short-term distractions.

2. Cultivating Patience:
- **Understanding the Long Game:** Develop an understanding that wealth-building is a long-term endeavor. Patience is the key to allowing investments to grow and compound over time.
- **Celebrating Milestones:** Acknowledge and celebrate smaller milestones along the way. This reinforces the idea that progress is being made, even if the ultimate goal is still distant.

3. Strategic Planning Amidst Short-Term Volatility:
- **Mitigating Short-Term Risks:** Implement strategies to mitigate the impact of short-term market volatility on your investments. Diversification and periodic rebalancing are essential tools.
- **Educate Yourself:** Enhance your understanding of market dynamics to make informed decisions during short-term fluctuations. Education builds confidence and reduces the impact of market noise.

4. Building Resilience:
- **Embracing Setbacks as Learning Opportunities:** View setbacks as learning opportunities rather than failures. This mindset shift builds resilience and prevents discouragement.
- **Adapting to Changes:** Cultivate adaptability in the face of unexpected challenges. Being flexible allows you to adjust your strategies without losing sight of long-term goals.

5. Maintaining Consistency:
- **Consistent Contributions:** Stick to a consistent schedule of contributions to your investment accounts. Regular investing, even in small amounts, accumulates over time and benefits from compounding.
- **Automated Financial Processes:** Automate financial processes such as contributions and bill payments. This reduces the need for constant manual intervention, ensuring consistency.

6. Focus on Value, Not Market Noise:
- **Avoiding Short-Term Market Hype:** Resist the temptation to react to short-term market hype or sensationalized news. Base decisions on long-term fundamentals rather than momentary market sentiment.
- **Selective Information Consumption:** Be selective in the information you consume. Focusing on quality sources and avoiding constant monitoring of short-term market movements reduces anxiety.

7. Regular Goal Reviews and Adjustments:
- **Periodic Goal Assessments:** Regularly review your long-term goals. Assess whether they remain aligned with your evolving priorities and make adjustments as necessary.
- **Flexible Planning:** Embrace the concept of flexible planning. Long-term goals may evolve, and being open to adjustments ensures continued relevance.

8. Building a Support System:
- **Surrounding Yourself with Like-Minded Individuals:** Cultivate a support system of individuals who share similar financial goals. This network provides encouragement and accountability.
- **Professional Guidance:** Seek professional financial guidance when needed. A financial advisor can offer insights and strategies to keep your long-term goals on track.

9. Mindfulness and Stress Management:
- **Mindfulness Practices:** Incorporate mindfulness practices into your routine. Techniques such as meditation and mindfulness help manage stress and maintain focus.
- **Balancing Well-being:** Recognize the interconnectedness of financial and mental well-being. Striking a balance ensures holistic success in both aspects.

10. Reviewing Long-Term Vision:
- **Revisiting Vision Statements:** If you have crafted a vision statement for your financial journey, revisit it regularly. This reaffirms your long-term vision and keeps it at the forefront of your mind.
- **Aligning Daily Actions with Vision:** Ensure that your daily financial actions align with your long-term vision. This conscious alignment reinforces commitment to the ultimate goals.

Conclusion: Nurturing Long-Term Success:
- **Persistence and Adherence:** Conclude by emphasizing the value of persistence and adherence to the long-term financial plan. The journey may have challenges, but staying focused on the destination ensures enduring success.

Staying focused on long-term goals requires a combination of strategic planning, mindset cultivation, and adaptability.

Decision-Making During Market Volatility: Navigating Uncertainty with Confidence

Market volatility is an inherent aspect of investing, and making sound decisions during periods of fluctuation is crucial for long-term financial success. This chapter explores strategies and principles to empower individuals to make informed decisions, stay resilient, and capitalize on opportunities amidst market turbulence.

1. Embracing a Long-Term Perspective:
- **Understanding Market Cycles:** Develop a deep understanding of market cycles. Recognize that short-term volatility is often a part of a broader cycle and should not dictate long-term investment decisions.
- **Reaffirming Long-Term Goals:** Regularly reaffirm your long-term financial goals. This perspective helps contextualize short-term market movements within the broader journey toward your objectives.

2. Avoiding Emotional Reactivity:
- **Staying Calm Amidst Fluctuations:** Cultivate emotional resilience to stay calm during market fluctuations. Emotional decision-making can lead to impulsive actions that may not align with long-term goals.
- **Implementing Waiting Periods:** Institute waiting periods before making significant decisions during volatile times. This provides a buffer to allow emotions to subside and rational thinking to prevail.

3. Dollar-Cost Averaging Strategies:
- **Consistent Contribution Plans:** Leverage dollar-cost averaging by maintaining consistent contribution plans. This strategy involves regularly investing a fixed amount, regardless of market conditions, reducing the impact of short-term price movements.
- **Systematic Buying Opportunities:** View market downturns as potential buying opportunities. Dollar-cost averaging allows you to accumulate more shares when prices are lower.

4. Diversification as a Risk Mitigation Tool:
- **Benefits of Diversification:** Reaffirm the importance of a well-diversified portfolio. Diversification helps spread risk across various asset classes, reducing the impact of volatility on the overall portfolio.
- **Rebalancing Strategies:** Periodically rebalance your portfolio to maintain the desired asset allocation. This involves selling assets that have performed well and reallocating funds to underperforming areas.

5. Selective Information Consumption:
- **Quality over Quantity:** Be discerning in the information you consume during volatile periods. Focus on quality sources that provide insights into the fundamentals of investments rather than reacting to sensationalized news.
- **Avoiding Market Noise:** Steer clear of excessive market noise. Constantly monitoring short-term movements can lead to overreaction and undermine long-term investment strategies.

6. Capitalizing on Volatility Opportunities:
- **Identifying Undervalued Assets:** Train yourself to identify potentially undervalued assets during market downturns. Such assets may present opportunities for long-term gains when markets stabilize.
- **Strategic Asset Allocation:** Adjust your asset allocation strategically to take advantage of asset classes that historically perform well during volatile periods.

7. Revisiting Risk Tolerance and Investment Plan:
- **Evaluating Risk Tolerance:** Reassess your risk tolerance periodically. Understand that risk tolerance can change, and it's crucial to ensure that your investment plan aligns with your current risk comfort level.
- **Adjusting Investment Plans:** Based on the reassessment, make adjustments to your investment plan if necessary. This may involve modifying asset allocations or exploring alternative investment strategies.

8. Seeking Professional Guidance:
- **Consulting Financial Advisors:** Engage with financial advisors during volatile times. Professional guidance provides a valuable external perspective and can help you make well-informed decisions aligned with your goals.
- **Leveraging Expertise:** Utilize the expertise of professionals to navigate complex market scenarios. Financial advisors can offer insights into potential opportunities and risks.

9. Preparing for Liquidity Needs:
- **Emergency Fund and Liquidity:** Prioritize liquidity needs and maintain an adequate emergency fund. This ensures that short-term financial needs can be met without the necessity of selling investments at inopportune times.
- **Balancing Liquidity and Investment Growth:** Strike a balance between maintaining liquidity and optimizing investment growth. This dual approach safeguards against unforeseen financial challenges.

10. Continuous Learning and Adaptation:
- **Educational Engagement:** Stay engaged in continuous learning about market dynamics and investment strategies. Education empowers you to adapt to evolving market conditions and make informed decisions.
- **Adapting to Changing Circumstances:** Cultivate adaptability as an investor. Markets evolve, and the ability to adapt your strategies to changing circumstances is essential for long-term success.

Conclusion: Navigating Volatility with Confidence:
- **Resilience and Confidence:** Conclude by emphasizing the importance of resilience and confidence in navigating market volatility. Sound decision-making,

coupled with a long-term perspective, positions you for financial success even in turbulent times.

Decision-making during market volatility requires a blend of rationality, adaptability, and a commitment to long-term financial goals

Capitalizing on Opportunities: Strategic Investing in Dynamic Markets

In dynamic and ever-changing financial markets, recognizing and capitalizing on opportunities is a key skill for investors seeking to maximize their returns. This chapter explores strategies and principles to help individuals identify, evaluate, and leverage opportunities effectively, fostering financial growth and resilience.

1. Vigilant Market Monitoring:
- **Stay Informed:** Maintain a vigilant approach to staying informed about market trends, economic indicators, and global events. Regularly monitor financial news, industry reports, and emerging trends.
- **Technological Tools:** Leverage technological tools and financial platforms that provide real-time data and analysis. Automation and data-driven insights can enhance your ability to identify opportunities swiftly.

2. Fundamental Analysis:
- **Company Fundamentals:** Conduct thorough fundamental analysis of potential investment opportunities. Evaluate a company's financial health, earnings potential, competitive positioning, and growth prospects.
- **Industry Trends:** Consider broader industry trends that may impact specific companies. Understanding the industry landscape provides context for assessing individual investment opportunities.

3. Technical Analysis:
- **Price Patterns and Trends:** Use technical analysis to identify price patterns and trends in asset prices. Chart analysis can help determine potential entry and exit points for trades or investments.
- **Indicators and Oscillators:** Explore technical indicators and oscillators that signal potential shifts in market sentiment. These tools can assist in timing investment decisions.

4. Opportunistic Asset Allocation:
- **Diversified Portfolio Approach:** Maintain a diversified portfolio that allows for opportunistic asset allocation. Allocate resources based on changing market conditions, emphasizing sectors or asset classes with growth potential.
- **Rebalancing Strategies:** Periodically rebalance your portfolio to align with changing market dynamics. Reallocating funds from overperforming to underperforming assets positions you to capitalize on emerging opportunities.

5. Crisis Investing:
- **Contrarian Approach:** Embrace a contrarian approach during market crises. Identify quality assets that may be undervalued due to market sentiment rather than intrinsic value.

- **Risk Mitigation:** Mitigate risks associated with crisis investing by conducting thorough due diligence. Analyze the financial stability and resilience of companies in times of economic downturns.

6. Sector Rotation Strategies:
- **Identifying Sector Trends:** Monitor sector trends and rotate investments based on economic cycles. Different sectors perform well at different phases of the economic cycle.
- **Cyclical and Defensive Allocations:** Adjust your portfolio with a mix of cyclical and defensive assets to align with economic conditions. Capitalize on sectors that thrive in both expansion and contraction phases.

7. ESG (Environmental, Social, and Governance) Investing:
- **Sustainable Growth Opportunities:** Explore opportunities in ESG investing, focusing on companies with strong environmental, social, and governance practices. Sustainable practices can contribute to long-term growth.
- **Aligning Values with Investments:** Align your values with your investments by considering ESG factors. This approach not only supports responsible investing but also identifies companies positioned for future success.

8. Emerging Markets and Innovations:
- **Exploring Emerging Markets:** Consider exposure to emerging markets that exhibit growth potential. These markets may offer unique opportunities not present in more established regions.
- **Innovative Technologies:** Explore investments in innovative technologies and industries. Disruptive technologies and new business models can create substantial growth opportunities.

9. Tactical Use of Options and Derivatives:
- **Hedging and Enhancing Returns:** Understand the tactical use of options and derivatives for both hedging and enhancing returns. Options can be employed to manage risk and take advantage of market volatility.
- **Risk Assessment:** Exercise caution and conduct thorough risk assessments when using options. Understand the potential downsides and employ strategies that align with your risk tolerance.

10. Networking and Professional Insights:
- **Networking in Financial Communities:** Engage with financial communities and networks. Exchange insights with professionals, attend conferences, and participate in forums to gain valuable perspectives.
- **Professional Advice:** Seek advice from financial professionals, such as advisors and analysts. Their expertise and market knowledge can provide nuanced insights into potential opportunities.

Conclusion: Strategic Agility for Financial Growth:
- **Adapting to Market Dynamics:** Conclude by emphasizing the importance of strategic agility. The ability to adapt to evolving market dynamics, identify opportunities, and capitalize on them positions investors for long-term financial growth.

Capitalizing on opportunities requires a combination of proactive market awareness, strategic planning, and a willingness to explore innovative investment avenues.

Resilience in Economic Downturns: Navigating Financial Challenges with Strength

Economic downturns are inevitable in the cyclical nature of economies. Building resilience during these periods is crucial for individuals to navigate financial challenges and emerge stronger. This chapter explores strategies and principles to foster financial resilience, enabling individuals to weather economic downturns with confidence.

1. Establishing an Emergency Fund:
- **Fundamentals of Emergency Funds:** Emphasize the importance of having a robust emergency fund. This fund serves as a financial buffer during unexpected events, providing a safety net for essential expenses.
- **Size and Accessibility:** Guide individuals in determining the appropriate size of their emergency fund, considering factors like monthly expenses, lifestyle, and job stability. Ensure the fund is easily accessible in times of urgency.

2. Prudent Debt Management:
- **Assessing and Prioritizing Debts:** Encourage individuals to assess their outstanding debts and prioritize repayment. Prioritizing high-interest debts helps reduce financial strain during economic downturns.
- **Negotiating with Creditors:** Advise on open communication with creditors. In times of financial hardship, negotiating revised payment plans or interest rates can provide temporary relief.

3. Budgetary Discipline:
- **Reviewing and Adjusting Budgets:** Stress the importance of budgetary discipline. Regularly review and adjust budgets to align with changing economic conditions, focusing on essential expenses.
- **Cutting Non-Essential Spending:** During economic downturns, recommend cutting non-essential spending. Temporarily eliminating discretionary expenses can free up funds for crucial financial priorities.

4. Diversified Income Streams:
- **Exploring Multiple Income Sources:** Encourage the exploration of diversified income streams. Having multiple sources of income provides a layer of protection during economic uncertainties.
- **Side Businesses and Freelancing:** Explore opportunities for side businesses or freelancing. These endeavors can supplement income and offer additional financial security.

5. Continuous Skill Development:
- **Adapting to Market Needs:** Highlight the importance of continuous skill development. Acquiring new skills or enhancing existing ones increases employability and adaptability in evolving job markets.
- **Online Courses and Certifications:** Promote the availability of online courses and certifications. These resources enable individuals to upskill from the comfort of their homes.

6. Insurance Coverage:
- **Comprehensive Insurance Policies:** Advocate for comprehensive insurance coverage. This includes health insurance, property insurance, and disability insurance to protect against unforeseen events and mitigate financial risks.
- **Regular Policy Reviews:** Stress the need for regular reviews of insurance policies. Ensure coverage aligns with current needs and consider adjustments as circumstances evolve.

7. Strategic Investment Planning:
- **Long-Term Investment Mindset:** Reinforce a long-term investment mindset. Discourage impulsive decisions driven by short-term market fluctuations and emphasize the benefits of staying committed to long-term goals.
- **Rebalancing and Diversification:** Encourage portfolio rebalancing and diversification. These strategies help manage risk and ensure a balanced approach to investments.

8. Government Assistance Programs:
- **Awareness of Available Programs:** Inform individuals about government assistance programs. During economic downturns, various support programs may provide temporary financial relief.
- **Eligibility and Application Process:** Provide guidance on determining eligibility and navigating the application process for government assistance. Timely access to these resources can ease financial burdens.

9. Community Support and Networking:
- **Community Resources:** Highlight the availability of local community resources. Food banks, counseling services, and job assistance programs can offer valuable support during challenging times.
- **Networking for Opportunities:** Encourage networking within local communities. Sharing experiences, resources, and job opportunities can create a supportive network during economic downturns.

10. Mental Health and Well-being:
- **Stress Management Practices:** Emphasize the importance of mental health. Recommend stress management practices such as exercise, mindfulness, and seeking professional support when needed.
- **Maintaining a Positive Outlook:** Encourage maintaining a positive outlook. Resilience goes beyond financial aspects and includes mental well-being, which plays a crucial role in navigating challenges.

Conclusion: Building Lasting Financial Resilience:
- **Holistic Approach:** Conclude by reinforcing the idea of a holistic approach to financial resilience. Building lasting financial resilience involves a combination of financial preparedness, adaptability, and maintaining overall well-being.

Building resilience in economic downturns is not just about weathering the storm but emerging stronger on the other side.

Conclusion: Empowering Financial Mastery for a Lifetime

In the journey towards financial mastery, this comprehensive guide has equipped individuals with the knowledge, tools, and strategies to take control of their financial destinies. From creating a personalized portfolio to navigating economic challenges and capitalizing on opportunities, each chapter has been meticulously crafted to guide readers through the intricate landscape of personal finance.

Foundations of Financial Empowerment:

- **Building a Solid Foundation:** Establishing a solid financial foundation is the first step towards empowerment. Readers have learned the importance of budgeting, emergency funds, and prudent debt management as pillars for financial stability.
- **Crafting a Personalized Portfolio:** The guide delved into the creation of a personalized portfolio, guiding readers through asset classes, stock selection, bond investments, and the strategic allocation of resources to align with individual goals and risk tolerance.

Navigating the Investment Landscape:
- **Understanding Asset Classes:** An in-depth exploration of asset classes, from stocks and bonds to cash and real estate, provided readers with a comprehensive understanding of the various investment options available.
- **Stocks: Ownership and Growth:** The guide elucidated the dynamics of stock ownership, growth strategies, and presented real case scenarios to illustrate the practicalities of investing in dividend stocks.
- **Bonds: Fixed Income and Stability:** Readers gained insights into the world of bonds, understanding the significance of credit ratings, and receiving guidance on when to consider corporate or government bonds.
- **Cash: Liquidity and Safety:** The chapter on cash emphasized the role of liquidity and safety in financial planning, highlighting the importance of having accessible funds for emergencies.

Diversification and Constructing Portfolios:
- **Importance of Diversification:** Diversification emerged as a fundamental principle, with readers learning the basics and rules to achieve a well-diversified portfolio that balances risk and reward.
- **Constructing Your Portfolio:** The guide provided a detailed roadmap for constructing portfolios, covering specific investments, asset allocation strategies, and the critical aspect of conducting thorough research before making investment decisions.

Tailoring Portfolios for Different Life Stages:
- **Portfolio Construction for a 30-Year-Old:** The step-by-step guide tailored a portfolio for a 30-year-old, considering asset classes, stocks, bonds, and specific recommendations for a robust financial foundation.
- **Portfolio Transition for a 60-Year-Old:** Transitioning to the needs of a 60-year-old close to retirement, the guide demonstrated adjustments in asset allocations, investments, and the importance of balance between growth and stability.

Strategies for Long-Term Success:
- **Staying Focused on Long-Term Goals:** The guide emphasized the significance of maintaining focus on long-term financial goals, providing strategies to navigate short-term distractions and market volatility.
- **Monitoring and Adjusting Your Portfolio:** Strategies for monitoring performance, rebalancing, and adapting to changing circumstances were explored, providing readers with tools to ensure their portfolios align with evolving goals.

Navigating Economic Challenges:
- **Addressing Economic Downturns:** In the face of economic downturns, readers learned to build resilience through emergency funds, prudent debt management, and adaptability in adjusting budgets and lifestyles.
- **Strategic Decision-Making During Volatility:** Decision-making during market volatility was addressed comprehensively, guiding readers on maintaining a long-term perspective, avoiding emotional reactivity, and capitalizing on opportunities.

Capitalizing on Opportunities:
  - **Strategic Investing in Dynamic Markets:** The chapter on capitalizing on opportunities equipped readers with the skills to identify and leverage

opportunities through vigilant market monitoring, fundamental and technical analysis, and strategic asset allocation.

Resilience in Economic Downturns:
- **Navigating Financial Challenges:** The guide provided a roadmap for navigating economic downturns, emphasizing the establishment of emergency funds, prudent debt management, and a holistic approach to building financial resilience.

Conclusion: A Lifetime of Financial Empowerment:
- **Holistic Financial Mastery:** In conclusion, this guide has endeavored to empower readers with the knowledge and skills to achieve financial mastery throughout their lifetimes.
- **Continued Learning and Adaptability:** The journey towards financial empowerment is ongoing, requiring continuous learning, adaptability, and a commitment to personal growth.
- **Navigate with Confidence:** Armed with the insights from this guide, readers are now equipped to navigate the complexities of personal finance with confidence, making informed decisions that align with their unique financial goals and aspirations.

Continuing Your Financial Education: A Lifelong Commitment to Knowledge
As you embark on your journey towards financial mastery, it's essential to recognize that learning is a continuous and dynamic process. The financial landscape evolves, and staying informed is crucial for making informed decisions. Here are strategies to continue your financial education:

- **Read Widely and Regularly:**
  - Diversify Your Reading List: Explore a wide range of financial literature, including books, articles, and reputable financial publications. This will provide diverse perspectives on market trends, investment strategies, and economic insights.
  - Stay Updated: Regularly read news updates, financial blogs, and market analyses to stay informed about current events and their potential impact on the financial world.
- **Engage in Online Courses and Webinars:**
  - Explore Online Learning Platforms: Enroll in online courses and webinars offered by reputable educational platforms. These resources cover various financial topics, from basic financial literacy to advanced investment strategies.
  - Attend Virtual Seminars: Participate in virtual seminars hosted by financial experts and institutions. These events often provide valuable insights and the opportunity to interact with industry professionals.
- **Leverage Educational Apps and Podcasts:**
  - Utilize Financial Apps: Download financial apps that offer educational content. Some apps provide interactive lessons on budgeting, investing, and financial planning.
  - Listen to Financial Podcasts: Tune into financial podcasts hosted by experts in the field. Podcasts offer an accessible and engaging way to stay informed while on the go.
- **Join Financial Communities and Forums:**

- Participate in Online Communities: Join online forums and communities where individuals discuss personal finance, share experiences, and seek advice. Engaging in conversations with peers can provide valuable insights and different perspectives.
- Follow Influential Figures: Follow financial experts, economists, and influencers on social media platforms. Many share timely updates, market analyses, and educational content that can enhance your understanding of financial concepts.

- **Consider Formal Education:**
- Pursue Higher Education: If you have a keen interest in finance, consider pursuing formal education such as a degree or certification in finance, economics, or a related field. This can deepen your understanding and open doors to more advanced career opportunities.
- Attend Workshops and Conferences: Attend workshops and conferences organized by educational institutions or industry associations. These events often feature experts and thought leaders sharing their knowledge on contemporary financial topics.

- **Network with Financial Professionals:**
- Build a Professional Network: Connect with financial professionals, advisors, and mentors. Networking provides opportunities to learn from experienced individuals, seek guidance on specific financial matters, and stay updated on industry trends.
- Participate in Industry Events: Attend industry conferences and events where you can network with professionals in the financial sector. Building relationships can lead to valuable insights and potential collaborations.

- **Continuously Assess Your Portfolio:**
- Regular Portfolio Reviews: Periodically review your investment portfolio. Assess the performance of your investments, consider rebalancing, and stay informed about changes in market conditions.
- Learn from Investment Decisions: Reflect on your past investment decisions, both successes and challenges. Understand the factors that influenced outcomes and use these lessons to refine your future strategies.

- **Stay Adaptable to Technological Advances:**
- Embrace Technological Tools: Stay abreast of technological advancements in finance. Explore new investment platforms, robo-advisors, and financial apps that can streamline your financial management and decision-making processes.
- Understand Cryptocurrencies and Fintech: Familiarize yourself with emerging technologies such as cryptocurrencies and financial technology (fintech). Understanding these innovations will contribute to a more comprehensive understanding of the evolving financial landscape.

- **Seek Professional Guidance:**
- Consult Financial Advisors: If needed, consult with financial advisors for personalized guidance. Professionals can provide tailored advice based on your financial situation, goals, and risk tolerance.
- Continuous Dialogue: Maintain an ongoing dialogue with your financial advisor. Regular discussions will ensure that your financial plan evolves to align with changes in your life circumstances and market conditions.

- **Stay Curious and Inquisitive:**

- Cultivate a Curious Mindset: Approach financial education with a curious and inquisitive mindset. Stay hungry for knowledge, be open to new ideas, and challenge your existing beliefs to foster continuous growth.
- Set Learning Goals: Establish learning goals for yourself, whether it's mastering a specific financial concept, understanding a particular investment strategy, or staying informed about global economic trends.

Continuing your financial education is not just a choice; it's a commitment to your financial well-being and success. By staying informed, embracing new knowledge, and adapting to changes, you empower yourself to navigate the dynamic world of finance with confidence and mastery.

Recommended Books:
- **"The Intelligent Investor" by Benjamin Graham:** A timeless classic that provides insights into value investing and building a solid investment philosophy.
- **"Rich Dad Poor Dad" by Robert T. Kiyosaki:** A foundational book on personal finance, focusing on mindset, assets, and building wealth.
- **"A Random Walk Down Wall Street" by Burton G. Malkiel:** A comprehensive guide to different investment strategies and the principles of financial markets.
- **"Your Money or Your Life" by Vicki Robin and Joe Dominguez:** Explores the relationship between money and life, offering practical advice on achieving financial independence.

- **"The Total Money Makeover" by Dave Ramsey:** A step-by-step guide to getting out of debt, building an emergency fund, and creating a solid financial plan.

Online Tools and Platforms:
- **Personal Capital:** A comprehensive financial management tool that tracks expenses, analyzes investment portfolios, and provides retirement planning tools.
- **Mint:** A budgeting app that helps you track spending, set financial goals, and get a holistic view of your financial health.
- **Robinhood:** A user-friendly investment platform that offers commission-free trading of stocks, ETFs, options, and cryptocurrencies.
- **Wealthfront:** A robo-advisor platform that provides automated, low-cost investment management and financial planning services.
- **YNAB (You Need A Budget):** A budgeting app that focuses on giving every dollar a job, helping users take control of their finances and save for future goals.

Financial Planning Services:
- **Vanguard Personal Advisor Services:** Combines automated investing with access to financial advisors, offering personalized investment strategies.
- **Betterment:** A robo-advisor platform that provides automated portfolio management, financial planning, and retirement savings advice.
- **Fidelity Wealth Services:** Offers a range of financial planning services, including investment management, retirement planning, and estate planning.
- **Charles Schwab Intelligent Portfolios:** A robo-advisor service that creates and manages a diversified portfolio based on individual goals and risk tolerance.
- **Ellevest:** A financial planning platform designed for women, offering goal-based investing and personalized advice.

Investment Research Websites:
- **Morningstar:** Provides in-depth analysis and ratings of mutual funds, stocks, and ETFs, helping investors make informed decisions.
- **Seeking Alpha:** A platform for stock market analysis, offering crowd-sourced research, news, and financial analysis.
- **Bloomberg:** A global financial news platform with comprehensive coverage of markets, economics, and business.
- **Yahoo Finance:** Offers a wide range of financial information, including stock quotes, news, and in-depth market analysis.
- **CNBC:** A leading financial news source that provides real-time market updates, expert commentary, and in-depth financial analysis.

www.ingramcontent.com/pod-product-compliance
Lightning Source LLC
Chambersburg PA
CBHW050117230526
45470CB00004B/1875